NAVIGATING THE QUARTERLIFE CAREER CRISIS

Real Stress, **Real** Solutions

NAVIGATING THE QUARTERLIFE CAREER CRISIS

Real Stress, **Real** Solutions

SCOTT DOYNE ICF ACC, MBA
Author of the *Career Crisis Series*

Published by Ripples Media

www.ripples.media

Atlanta, GA

Copyright © 2026 by Scott Doyne

All rights reserved. No part of this book may be reproduced or used in any manner without written permission of the copyright owner except for the use of quotations in a book review. For more information: publishing@ripples.media

First printing 2026

www.scottdoyne.com

Headshot photo on back cover by Sophie Doyne (@bysophiedoyne)

Cover design & book interior by Carolyn Asman

ISBN 978-1-971718-01-9 Paperback

ISBN 978-1-971718-02-6 Hardback

ISBN 978-1-971718-00-2 E-book

Library of Congress Control Number: 2026904378

To the next generation,
including my favorite Quarterlifers,
Brandon and Sophie

Contents

Foreword IX

Preface 15

Introduction 19

Section 1 Career Stressors 31
Fear of Failure 33
Career Path Uncertainty 45
Feeling Stuck or Lost 57

Section 2 Career Stress Solutions 65
Stress Relief 67
Mentoring 79
Networking 89

Section 3 The Job Search 99
Finding a Job/Internship 101
College Career Resources 115

Section 4 Bad News/Good News 131
Social Media 133
Artificial Intelligence 143
Family 153

Section 5 Adulting 165
Reality Check 167
Financial Stress .177
Religion, Faith and Spirituality 187

World Events 197
Entrepreneurship 203

Section 6 Career Coaching 213
What is Coaching? .215

Conclusion 221

Acknowledgments 225

Endnotes 227

Research Appendix 237

Consolidated Resources 241

Exercises 244

About the Author 251

Foreword

by Rennie Curran

Keynote Speaker, Author of *Free Agent*, Executive Coach, Former University of Georgia and NFL Linebacker

There is always a moment in everyone's life where the play we've been running, in your life and career, suddenly stops working. For most of us this happens right around the time when you reach a major milestone and everyone expects you to "have it all together."

No matter what stage you find yourself, you're supposed to know what you're doing, where you're going, and who you're becoming in that phase of life. In your mind you're supposed to look confident, even if you have no blueprint to follow. The same questions usually come up, like: *Am I on the right track? Did I make the right decision? What if I fail? What If I succeed, but can't sustain it? What if I waste all this time chasing something what wasn't meant for me?*

If that's you, I want you to hear me and hear me clearly. You're not lost. You're not behind. You're not alone.

I've had more than enough experiences in my personal and professional life, coaching tons of leaders and high performers, to know that fear and anxiety doesn't show up when you're weak- minded. Many times it results from the fact that you care. You have standards. You're not OK with settling or wasting your talent. You feel the unexplainable weight of expectations from family, peers, society, and those who came before you.

When you're in those formative years, that weight can feel unbearable; nothing you do lightens the load. The hardest part is when everything looks good on the outside. You made it to the good college that everyone knows. You might have even graduated and gotten the job that everyone sees as a success. You're doing everything right, but you still feel uncertain, insecure, stuck, and unfulfilled. The mental discomfort between where you are and where you see yourself in your mind can be extremely irritating.

That's exactly why I love this book.

It doesn't just dismiss what you're feeling and give you motivational messages with no substance. It identifies real issues and provides you with real solutions, not just theoretical research. It's practical, straight to the point, and relevant for the everyday person. It can be a game changer if you apply the advice given in the book.

As someone who has navigated several major transitions in life, shifting from an athlete to entrepreneurship, learning to rebuild my belief after a major setback, and having to learn to maintain self-motivation when the cheering stops, I know all about what comes with that transformation.

As a father and public figure, I'm familiar with the pressure and expectations to have it all figured out. It can steal your joy, stifle your progress, and destroy your sense of self-worth if you don't learn how to manage it.

This is why I appreciate Scott's approach in this book. He doesn't pretend to have all the answers. Instead, he helps you break things down mentally by posing the right questions, understanding that better assessments lead to better decisions and ultimately better outcomes. After reading this book you will feel empowered and challenged in a good way.

You are reminded that failure isn't an attack on your character—it's just feedback. You begin to understand that there's no such thing as a straight line when it comes to your career. The focus centers on progress, repetition, and adaptability.

You'll learn how to manage stress while honoring your true identity, how to build relationships that are mutually beneficial, and how to network in an authentic way.

Thinking clearly in a world full of noise is a crucial takeaway from this book. There are so many distractions, whether it's social media, family, peers, world events, and comparing ourselves to each other. That noise prevents you from having clarity and the less clarity you have, the less confidence you will possess.

As you read this book, I want to provide you with four pieces of advice:

> **1. Take the time to reflect** – One of the strongest things you can do is to be real about where you are and what you're carrying. Don't try to be perfect. It's OK to have fear, uncertainty, and frustration. Get all of the negative thoughts and beliefs out of your mind through journaling.
>
> **2. Start with small steps** – Even if those initial strides aren't perfect, clarity comes from consistent action. You'll never be able to think your way into success. It will come one rep, one conversation, one event, one application, at a time. If you can commit to not just reaching for an outcome, but ensuring it becomes part of your routine, you'll be surprised at all the good things that will happen.
>
> **3. Build your team** – Isolation will always lead to anxiety and frustration. Being in the right community

of trusted advisors can help you remain grounded and maintain the right perspective. A mentor can help you avoid pitfalls and accelerate progress through just one referral or recommendation.

4. Remember to be more than just a title – Your job is not who you are, it's just what you do. Your bank account does not define your self-worth. Your current season, no matter how bad, is temporary. Years from now this challenge will be the very thing that leads to your success and your ability to lead others.

As you take the time to read, make sure you reflect, take notes, and, most of all, take action! Apply the good and leave the bad.

Don't forget to celebrate the wins! The fact that you are choosing to learn, manage stress, and take initiative in your life already puts you ahead of the game. You don't have to have everything figured out, but you just need to be willing to try and keep putting your best foot forward.

This book will assist you in doing just that. Wishing you continued success on your journey!

Preface

> *Quarterlife is a pivotal time in people's lives, a time of acceptance, and an invitation of trial and error.*
>
> Haleigh, 24-year-old marketer in Connecticut[1]

Alright, so let's get something out of the way here—I'm now 51 years old. What do I know about the life of an 18- to 25-year-old? Well, I'm not a Boomer; I'm Gen X. My kids are Gen Z, and I'm inspired by Gen Alpha. I promise not to attempt the slang of your generation. I've made that mistake before and found that the best approach to communicating with young professionals is to ask questions, listen more, and talk less. So that's what I've done while writing this book.

In my professional career as a sports media executive at Turner Broadcasting, I always sought perspective from younger employees to get their take on what we should be developing for our fans. As I was leading digital businesses on behalf of NASCAR and the NBA, our mandate was to innovate and drive maximum engagement with younger fans. In addition, I was often called upon to help with employee onboarding, participate in internal panel discussions with junior staff, and provide a variety of opportunities to support emerging leaders.

Throughout my life, I embraced the next generation. I have been a youth sports coach, a Big Brother, a manager, a mentor, a teacher, and I'm now a career coach with over 1,000 hours of sessions complete, including more than a third of my time spent with young professionals under the age of 30. After a successful 25-year corporate career, coaching has undoubtedly become my calling, and I am honored by the opportunity to help people help themselves every single day.

With that said, my empathy is most present in my number-one job—being a parent. I am the proud father of adult children now ages 20 and 22, and I am keenly aware of the many challenges they face as they pursue their own life goals and career paths. The job market and society at large are way more complicated than when I was your age. Even so, I believe my kids have more advantages than many who are their same ages, so I'll prioritize addressing you from my professional point of view, as objectively as possible, considering the wide range of experiences you all represent.

For the past three years, I've taught college seniors at Emory University a course on career navigation, leveraging many of the career-coaching frameworks I use with my clients. Every year, students say they wish they had learned these career search skills sooner, even as freshmen or before. *Navigating the Quarterlife Career Crisis* is my attempt to help you survive and thrive through your late teens and early 20s into adulthood. This includes deciding on your path through college (or not), building relevant skills, and finding internships and jobs amid today's crazy world, with AI proliferation and the pressures that come with adulting. Most of all, I am here to help you find ways to manage your stress throughout all of those big life situations.

My promise to you is this: **if you can reduce your career anxiety, then you will have a more fulfilling life.**

Introduction

Imagine that you just turned 30. You have a roof over your head, a car that works, good friends, and a steady income. And you're happy. Not bad, right?

You didn't get there easily, though. There were some bumps in the road. Hurdles. Setbacks. You have the scars to prove it. But after a few years, you're kinda getting the hang of this thing called life. You figured it out.

You can hear me now and believe me later—you can do this! Billions of young people have survived adolescence and adulting before you. Your challenges might be unique, but so are your strength, your courage, and your ability to overcome any obstacles in your way.

This book began as my previous book was in progress. *Exploring the Midlife Career Crisis* consumed much of my headspace from 2020 until the publish date of September 24, 2024—my 50th birthday. With that symbolic step, I put the pain of a recent layoff behind me and catapulted towards a new calling.

During that process, I found myself thinking further back in my career—how it all started, where my journey began. I documented some of those early chapters and set them aside for an intended prequel—*The Quarterlife Career Crisis*. It was originally envisioned as an autobiography, a tale that would be told about my teenage tribulations leading into my mid-twenties ... athletic heartbreak, academic reckoning, and a dream deferred.

But that's not what this book is about.

Initial drafts eventually led me somewhere unexpected, more powerful, and full of purpose I didn't know I had in me. This book isn't about *my* quarterlife career crisis. **It's about yours.** Your stress, your fears, your job hunt ... and your future.

When is Quarterlife?

When I asked that question to a group of 18- to 25-year-olds, I got the same response just about every time—a blank stare, a little thought, then they said with a quizzical guess—"25?" It was like they had never contemplated the question before.

At your age, thinking about your life in quadrants might feel silly, or even irrelevant. I'm not referencing *quarter-life* to stress you out, actually just the opposite. I want to remind you that you have time. You will grow. You will learn. You will achieve. Of course, you will have challenges along the way, but you will also have amazing experiences you haven't even dreamed of yet.

As a matter of calculation, 25 isn't a bad guess at all. Based on the most recent data from the National Vital Statistics System, life expectancy for the U.S. population in 2023 was 78.4. For females specifically, it's risen to 81.1. Furthermore, if you reach 65, your average lifespan now extends towards 85.[2]

I probably don't need to tell you that aging isn't promised. You likely have someone in your life who has passed away prior to the age these statistical norms suggest. I'm now 51 and have already lost multiple high school friends before their expected time—one to a sudden aneurism and another to suicide. I have also seen two of my business school friends bury their teenage children—unthinkable tragedies. I don't want you to dwell on this kind of heartache, so instead I'll ask you, **what would you want to do today, if you knew there wasn't a tomorrow?**

Let's look at the numbers a different way ... instead of calculating a percentage of your total life, we can look at the portion of your adult life you have already completed. Let's take a 20-year-old as an example. You are two years past your 18th birthday and therefore only three percent of your way to age 80. Even if you want to retire at 60, you're still less than five percent of the way from age 18 to that point.

Age 20 is less than 5% of your expected adult working lifespan

With this optimism in mind, you can absolutely still seize the day, but you can also breathe for a second and realize that what you do today won't determine everything that happens for the rest of your life. There will be time for adjustment, adaptation, and new decisions based on new information.

What is a Career Crisis?

Nevaeh is a 22-year-old master's degree student in Portland, Oregon, who says, "My career right now is busy, hectic, messy, and tiring."[3]

One recent graduate, Haleigh, explains her career crisis at this age as a result of making a series of important decisions for herself for the first time, "It comes fast. Basically, once we graduate high school, let's decide if we're going to college, which college we go to, what our major is. Then internships, then what our first job will look like. So just a lot of decision making that happens in such a short period of time when we haven't really been exposed to that much decision making prior to that."

I surveyed hundreds of 18- to 25-year-olds as I was doing research for this book. The research illustrates career stress as the number one type of stress reported in that survey, with only financial stress coming in a very close second. The other causes of stress didn't land anywhere close on the scale.[4]

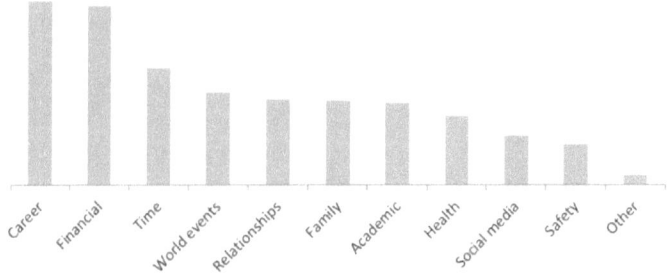

Main causes of overall stress
(among 18-25 year olds)

Your concerns are not unfounded, backed by some trends I've gathered when researching this age group:

- Hiring for college graduates in 2025 was down 16 percent compared to 2024 and 44 percent below 2022 levels.[5]
- More than half of college seniors feel pessimistic about starting their careers because they worry about a competitive job market and a lack of job security.[6]

- Gen Z workers are more likely than their older peers to worry they will lose their job or their job will be eliminated by generative AI.[7]
- 62 percent of young adults say they aren't employed in the career they intended to pursue after graduation.[8]

You are not alone with your worries. According to LinkedIn research, 75 percent of 25- to 33-year-olds have experienced quarterlife crises.[9] The most common feelings reported in this study of more than 6000 respondents are insecurity, uncertainty, disillusionment, loneliness, and identity confusion.

This feeling is legitimate and common:

- 12.6 million people between the ages of 18 and 25 experienced a mental, behavioral, or emotional health issue in the past year. This amounts to one in three (36.2 percent) young adults, a percentage that is higher than any other adult age range. This rate has increased significantly over the past several years (from 22.1 percent in 2016).[10]
- Among college students, 36 percent have been diagnosed with anxiety and 30 percent have been diagnosed with depression.[11]
- 42.7 percent of young adults ages 18 to 25 perceived an unmet need for mental health services.[12]

Throughout this book, you'll read heartfelt examples of your peers' stress spectrum, exacerbated by complex family and financial situations, and of course, by social media and COVID-19 implications.

As I dug deeper into my research, a variety of career-related stressors surfaced that I will explore throughout this book: career path uncertainty, finding a job/internship, financial pressure, feeling lost or stuck, among others. The chart below reflects the relative rankings of these competing pressures.[13] Which of these resonate most for you? We'll explore most of these in subsequent chapters, and will provide resources to help you out.

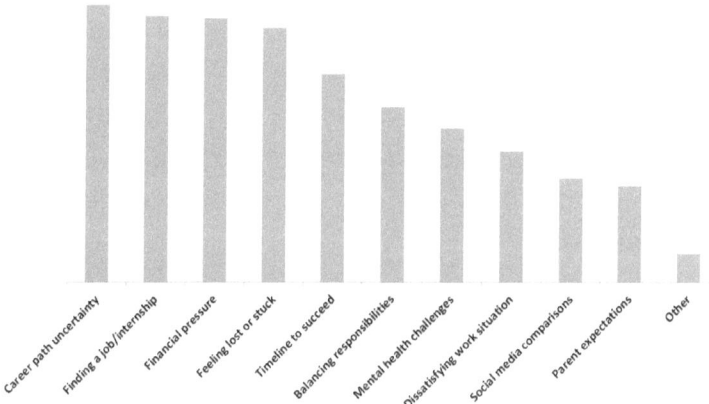

Main causes of career stress
(among 18-25 year olds)

My goal is to give your stressful struggles a voice, prove to you that you are not alone, and enable a communal swell of impact that has not been accomplished before.

The path you end up embracing is your own to choose, and I guarantee it will be different than anyone else's. This is your life, based on your dreams and your reality.

Before setting out on my own work, I inhaled the foundational efforts of many researchers, scholars, and fellow authors. I am indebted to them. Their insights have been a critical springboard to my efforts.

Two of my favorite authors are Adam Grant and Brene Brown. I believe the exceptional connection they have developed with their audience is, in part, a byproduct of great research—the desire and persistence to better understand human behavior, psychology, and motivation. As I set my mind to the topic of early career struggles, I knew I had to begin with research. I've now interviewed dozens of 18- to 25-year-olds and conducted a substantial survey to gather insights from hundreds more. What I discovered not only validated my hypothesis, but I also unearthed detailed, vulnerable, and thoughtful responses. And I hit the motherload of impactful resources and solutions—**by you, for you.**

With those suggestions in hand, I discovered a bevy of relevant resources from a network of existing stakeholders who share my passion for this cause. We stand ready to support you whenever you're ready, in whatever ways you need it. We are poised to help, not as nosy Gen Xers, Millennials, or Boomers telling you what to do. We are here as partners, ready and willing to help by listening to what you have to say and helping you achieve your wildest dreams.

In this book, you'll meet a host of characters: students, college graduates, soldiers, entrepreneurs, non-profit leaders, authors, parents, professors, university career center staff, mental health professionals, and many more. They all have a variety of perspectives on the quarterlife career crisis, and their points of view are valid. You may find yourself nodding your head in agreement with what one person says and disagreeing vigorously with somebody else. That's fine—I expect you to have your own unique reaction, because you have traveled a singular path and you will naturally gravitate towards a singular understanding of the world around you. That's what makes you special. That truth also allows you to leave space for new information, other perspectives, and therefore growth. As Adam Grant posted, "You can change your beliefs without changing your values."

In a way, this is still a sort of prequel to my midlife memoir. It's an attempt to plant a tree under whose shade I will not directly benefit, but it addresses your generation and possibly generations into the future. If I'm being honest, it's also a letter to my younger self. Challenging transitions are not owned by any age group or class, not anyone's domain or expertise. Even as we move past one tribulation, we are likely headed towards another, but every time that happens, we are more prepared than we were for the last.

Experience is the greatest teacher ... even failure for that matter. The benefit is not just your own, but your stories of overcoming challenges will be the greatest gift you will provide your future children and grandchildren, nieces and nephews, employees and mentees. Crisis is okay, and there are so many ways to overcome adversity that you are just beginning to develop—leaning on other people, leveraging available tools, building new skills, leveling up your attitude and aptitude.

As a quick tour of what you're about to experience, you'll first hear from your peers and experts on the key stress sources that arose from our research: fear of failure, career path uncertainty, and feeling stuck or lost. Before you get lost in a quagmire of conundrums, I'll unveil a set of key stress solutions, including practical paths towards mentoring and networking. We'll then move on to one of your biggest career questions: how to get a job or internship. And in some cases you might even discover unique resources on your college campus not limited to the official career office.

Before long, you'll be experiencing the double-edged swords of social media, artificial intelligence, and the duality of pressure and support that comes from family. From there, I'll join you on the adulting adventure, ending with the allure of entrepreneurship and an introduction to the benefits of coaching.

Lastly, all of the solutions and resources presented are also captured in a consolidated format at the end of the book as a convenient reference as you make your way through the twists and turns of your career journey.

One author's note I'd like to be clear about—while I have inserted verbatim excerpts that were captured during my research, I have maintained client confidentiality unless otherwise approved. As such, some of the quotes used represent the collective point of view of young professionals and cannot be extrapolated as prescriptive for any one reader.

So, before we get into the meat of this work, I'd like to invite you to picture a scenario ... you're lost, you're stuck, you're not sure if you picked the right major, and you don't know what to do next with your career. Ordinarily, that might send you into a tailspin of self-reliant independence. A downward spiral in your soul that refuses to loosen the vice grip on your heart or quiet the victim's voice in your head. An instinctual tendency to fight, flight, or freeze.

Instead ... take a moment ... *to breathe.*

The words from your contemporaries on the following pages will unlock something novel and mighty in your life—a newfound comfort with uncertainty, contentment with change, a light at the end of the tunnel, belief in yourself. I can't wait for you to hear what your peers have to say. Targeted advice, practical resources, genuinely caring organizations, and actual people who can help you navigate your own path through the jungle of job searching and career navigation in a way that you never thought was possible. Ready? Let's go!

Section 1

Career Stressors

CHAPTER 1
Fear of Failure

I thought the world had collapsed when I didn't get into Georgia Tech. That moment I thought, like, wow, I'm not going to succeed.

William, 27-year-old computer science graduate, Atlanta, Georgia[14]

Fuck failure. Seriously, I'm so tired of failure being looked at with such negativity. Failed projects, failed relationships, failed attempts are all SO much better than not even trying. As Tennyson said, "Tis better to have loved and lost than never to have loved at all."[15] I think risk-taking is awesome, and scary. I understand we all feared failing tests or classes in school, believing the false narrative that one F would destroy our futures. That must be where some of the habituation and stigma is formed. It just has to be eradicated. Are your parents to blame? Do they expect perfection? How unrealistic. Perfection is an illusion. Who even gets to judge how worthy you are, or your accomplishments?

I don't want to trivialize this, because the feeling is real. Some people have been punished, scorned, and forewarned that you only get one chance. I've heard this from many of my friends who are immigrant children or from strict African American families. Education is the way out! Get a degree, get perfect grades, then everything will work out for you! Oh man, a reality check is coming for anyone who thinks that is true. Your parents might even realize the torturous pressure this inflicts — it's generational and undeniable. But you can stop the forlorn legacy.

Should you be striving for something else? How about happiness and fulfillment? How about impact on society? I get it, becoming a doctor or lawyer is the ultimate parental brag point. *Look! My kid is a _____. Aren't you so impressed with me as a parent? Didn't I do such a great job?* My survey participants raised the concept of failure across a variety of situations including failed interviews, failed college classes, and failed job situations. Students consistently mention fear of failure as a major barrier to taking career risks.

Failing my first internship interview made me question everything.

20-year-old female college student, Dallas, Texas

I failed a class, and now I feel like my career is over before it started.

21-year-old male college student,
New Orleans, Louisiana

I'm scared of failing and letting my family down.

21-year-old male college student, Miami, Florida

Some of you may have seen the poignant press conference video of NBA Superstar Giannis Antetokounmpo where he talks about failure, following his team's 2nd Round elimination from the 2023 NBA Playoffs. In case you aren't familiar with him, Giannis is known as the "Greek Freak," a multi-time MVP and 2022 NBA Champion. He is as well known for his statistics as his ability to make a layup after only a few very long strides once he crosses halfcourt. He unwittingly became a spokesperson for redefining losing when he said, "There's no failure in sports ... it's steps to success. There's good days, bad days. Some days you are able to be successful, some days you are not."

He also looked back on the career of one of the GOATs of basketball saying: "Michael Jordan played 15 years, won six championships ... the other nine years was a failure?"

You really only have two options for this answer:

1. Yes, he was a failure, and that's okay.

2. No, he wasn't a failure as a person, he just failed to reach his goal those other nine years.

If MJ is a failure, then how could any of us be successful? We can aspire to lofty goals, but let's not beat ourselves up if we shoot for the stars and land on the moon. What do you think?

Your Saboteurs

One of the things I've learned a lot about as a coach is assessment. I was a psychology minor in college and have always been fascinated by how the brain works and why people act the way they do. Human behavior is driven by a unique combination of nature and nurture. I don't know the proportions, but there's no doubt that each plays a role in how people function.

One of the assessments that has been revealing to me and to my clients is called the Saboteur Assessment. It's part of a body of work by Shirzad Chamine, productized as "Positive Intelligence." Anyhow, the Saboteur Assessment identifies a list of characteristics that can be derailers based on how stress may show up in your daily actions or discussions.[16]

As described on their official website,

> *Saboteurs are the voices in your head that generate negative emotions as you handle life's everyday challenges.*

They represent the automatic patterns in your mind for how to think, feel, and respond. Your saboteurs cause all of your stress, anxiety, self-doubt, frustration, restlessness, and unhappiness. They sabotage your performance, well-being, and relationships. The Saboteur Assessment is your first step to conquering your saboteurs—identifying them to expose their lies and limiting beliefs.

For example, my top three saboteurs are Hyper-Achiever, People Pleaser, and Avoider. While they may come off as weaknesses, I don't see them that way. The hyper-achiever in me helps me push myself towards extraordinary outcomes. Ego aside, I want to be great. I want to make a difference. I have always wanted to exceed expectations and claim impressive accomplishments. That could lead others to a fear of failure, but for me, failure is a motivator. In my opinion, done is better than perfect. Trying is better than sitting on the sidelines. An error of commission is better than an error of omission.

As I look back at my high school years, I tended to gravitate toward the most difficult positions in every sport in which I competed. I pole vaulted on the track and field team, I swam the butterfly, and in football I was the punt and kick returner. In the rearview, I now realize this was bold and strategic. Nobody else wanted to take on those roles, and if I worked hard enough, I knew I could succeed.

With that said, I suffered a major shoulder injury during my junior year that took me away from all of it. It was personally painful, and I fell into a bit of a depression before I discovered a new path as a swim coach. That was my first fulfilling glimpse into a life of helping others succeed. I truly believe that heartbreak and the resulting light bulb eventually made me a better manager and career coach.

Early in my career, I had Teddy Roosevelt's *Man in the Arena* speech on my cubicle wall with the indelible clauses, "there is no effort without error and shortcoming." and "who at the worst, if he fails, at least fails while daring greatly, so that his place shall never be with those cold and timid souls who neither know victory nor defeat."[17]

If a president from the early 1900's isn't your speed, how about heeding the words of Oscar-winning actor Denzel Washington as he spoke to University of Pennsylvania graduates in 2011:

> **Fail big.** *That's right. Fail big ... It's a new world out there, and it's a mean world out there, and you only live once. So do what you feel passionate about. Take chances, professionally. Don't be afraid to fail. There's an old IQ test with nine dots, and you had to draw five lines with a pencil within these nine dots without lifting the pencil, and the only way to do it was to go outside the box. So don't be afraid to go outside the box.*[18]

Not to be left out, here are some timeless thoughts from Taylor Swift in her 2022 commencement speech at NYU:

My experience has been that my mistakes led to the best thing in my life. Being embarrassed when you mess up is part of the human experience of getting back up, dusting yourself off, and seeing who still wants to hang out with you afterward and laugh about it. That's a gift. The times I was told no or wasn't included, wasn't chosen, didn't win, didn't make the cut, looking back it really feels like those moments were as important if not more crucial than the moments I was told yes.[19]

The Path To The Path

One of my clients is an aspiring filmmaker, and he's legitimately making progress towards that goal. Reading scripts, writing scripts, networking with the right people. Does that mean he's going to be a showrunner before he's 30? Maybe not, but he's giving himself a chance while paying the bills with other income sources. As part of one of our recent coaching sessions, I sent him these notes as part of a list of Hollywood icons who traveled a long or curvy path to stardom:

- Quentin Tarantino spent years working at a video rental store in Manhattan Beach, where he obsessively watched films and developed his encyclopedic knowledge of cinema. He also worked as an usher at an adult theater and did various odd jobs before Reservoir Dogs launched his career.[20]
- Kevin Smith worked at a convenience store in New Jersey, which directly inspired his breakout film *Clerks* (1994). He famously maxed out credit cards

and sold his comic book collection to fund the $27,575 production, shooting at night in the actual store where he worked.²¹

- Donald Glover worked various jobs, including as a DJ and writer for comedy websites while developing his voice. He was still doing odd gigs when he got hired for *30 Rock*.²²
- Judd Apatow worked at a comedy club as a dishwasher as a way to learn from comics he looked up to.²³

The list could go on for many pages. Eventually, these directors often channeled their working-class experiences directly into their filmmaking, giving their early work an authentic, lived-in quality that helped distinguish them from film school graduates. Were they failing? Or were they learning?

Sometimes, in the words of author Dr. Willie Jolley, those setbacks are just the setup for a comeback. This even applies to my own family, if you'll allow me a proud #girldad moment. When my daughter was 10 years old, she tried out for the local soccer club. I'm not talking about recreational soccer … this was "serious" soccer. I know, how serious can it be for kids that just hit double digits? Well, if you're asking that, you haven't met competitive youth soccer girls (or their parents)!

Anyhow, to save you the trivial details, there are several levels of teams for each club and league, and Sophie did fine and got on a mid-level team. I actually think she would have been okay with it, except the other girls in her elementary school teased her for not being at their elevated level. Yes, pre-pubescent mean girls. It was awful to watch her shed tears over something like this.

As it turned out, she made great friends on her team and even got to play goalie for a pivotal penalty kick shootout in the season-ending tournament. I was nervous, but she wasn't, and she proceeded to stop several balls from crossing the goal line. Her team won the game and the championship. It's one of our favorite memories of her childhood athletic career, and she continued to play soccer throughout high school and even into college intramural as something that was fun for her and not the stressful experience of some other families at higher levels.

When she and I talked about the lessons learned from that season, I refer to it as the gold lining. As you're probably aware, a silver lining is when you try to see the positives from what seems like a bad situation. That's great, but what if a negative experience actually made your life better, richer for the challenge that you had conquered after hitting a roadblock?

This concept is a version of what's taught by the Stoics—the works of Socrates, Plato, and Aristotle. In the last decade, there's been a resurgence of interest in this philosophy, including a very popular book by Ryan Holiday, called *The Obstacle is the Way*. In that text, he suggests,"The obstacle in the path becomes the path. Never forget, **within every obstacle is an opportunity to improve our condition.**"[24]

In the 2023 *Paw Patrol* movie, Christina Aguilera sings a version of a song originally written by Tom Petty called "Learning to Fly." Here's an excerpt:

> *We all start at the beginning*
> *Unsure who we'll become*
> *And try to find a place to belong*
> *One day, you'll make it to your place in the sun.*

Later in the song is my favorite line—"*sometimes, even heroes have to wait.*" This essentially underscores the value of finding a balance between dreaming, action, and patience. I do believe you'll get where you are supposed to be ... it's just a matter of time.

Successful entrepreneur Daniel Debow who sold his company to Salesforce says, "Forget about your 'career path.' Embrace a career stumble." He relates, "My path was not a plan. It was a stumble. I just kept my eyes open, worked hard, and leaped at opportunities that excited me."[25]

One book I'd recommend in this vein is *Failureship*, by John Hartz, an entrepreneur, youth pastor, and three-time author. He says:

> *The world tells us to fear failure above all else. I would argue that this fear of failure, amid a culture that idolizes achievement, is the root cause of most of the anxiety and depression people experience each day. The humility that results from acknowledging our failures helps us get over ourselves so that we can be concerned for others.*

It provides empathy that helps us truly love others and serve them well.[26]

This isn't an "everybody gets a trophy" angle. Effort matters. Trying matters. I just think people will be more likely to go after something meaningful if they don't fear other people's judgment when they don't succeed. To me, the message is that **you can fail and still love yourself and be loved by others.** If I'm living life the way I want to, I fail every day. I failed to exercise as much as I wanted to. I failed to set ambitious revenue goals. I failed to write a better paragraph than this one ;).

Coaching Question: What is the best thing that could happen if you fail?

CHAPTER 2
Career Path Uncertainty

How am I supposed to know what I want to do the rest of my life?

21-year-old female college student
from Alabama

Why do you think you're supposed to have your entire life planned out before you turn 20? It's not your fault, but society is breathing down your neck with this preposterous expectation. It's bullshit. It's ridiculous. It's an illusion. And it's not necessary.

About 10 years ago, I was on a panel for an internal conference at my former company. The event was called "She's Got Game," specifically designed for college women who wanted to work in sports. In the Q&A session, a student who had driven to Atlanta from Alabama for the event stood up, and in the most desperate tone, asked the question at the beginning of this chapter. It hit me hard. In a way, that was the seminal reason I decided to write this book, to do my part to reduce the false need for certainty at such a young age.

For me, I could never have decided in college that I wanted to run NASCAR.com or NBA.com. Why? Because the internet as we know it didn't even exist yet! The same is going to be true for young people today. **The job you will have in a decade may not be a role in any company right now.** With the rapid and foundational changes happening in technology, new jobs, companies, and industries will develop, and you could be great in one of them! I like to think about career journeys as more of a compass than a turn-by-turn roadmap. It's enough to be pointed in the right direction. Really, any direction will do.

I promise you will learn so much from every experience that will come in handy later in your career. For now, instead of asking people what they want to be when they grow up, I ask them "What might you want to try next?" Based on that experience, you will learn, adapt, and grow.

And even if it's shitty, you will build character and resilience that can be leveraged long into the future.

The psychological desire for certainty makes a lot of sense. We are programmed to fear the unknown. Sameness feels comfortable. But it's also boring as hell. Do you really want to do the same thing over and over again the rest of your career? Tackling tedious tasks and going through the motions leads to absolute monotony. But really, uncertainty can be exciting. Anything can happen. You will likely get laid off at least once in your career. I know I have. And it's not a death sentence. It's a signal that it's time for something new. And it's absolutely possible that you'll like it better, maybe even love it. For me, that's how I discovered my new calling as a career coach.

According to a study by The Organization for Economic Cooperation and Development (OECD), "The proportion of students experiencing career uncertainty has increased by more than 50 percent since 2018."[27] Survey participants expressed uncertainty in career direction, often juggling multiple interests and unclear paths. When asked about future plans, "IDK" or "open to anything" appeared in 23 percent of survey answers. When it comes to choosing a major, nine percent of respondents said they are undecided on their major, and this group reported the highest stress among all respondents (8.6 out of 10).

As sadly stated by a 20-year-old from Florida, "The future feels like a giant question mark."

Even when choosing a major, current students seem to be unsure that it will lead to the job they actually want. Many in that situation suffer from perpetual waffling. One of the students I interviewed for this book told me, "I would say, my career right now is on four different paths, like, I'm on the fork on the road, and I'm like walking down one path, but going back and walking back another ... like, it's very multifaceted in a sense."

A 22-year-old recent college graduate in Chicago is also unsure she's on the right road, "Every time I think I've chosen a path, I second-guess myself."

Another recent college grad, a young woman from California, even fears getting the job she thought she wanted. "What if I get there in that career and I actually don't like it? What if I get that dream job, and then it's not for me?"

Do you feel this way? If so, there are plenty of logical reasons, and you are not alone. Desire for certainty is a natural reaction to the fear of the unknown. Control is also a common craving, especially for many high performers. Remember the Saboteur Assessment I mentioned in the Introduction? One of the most common saboteurs is called The Stickler. Many of my clients have this character trait. You might refer to it as being a perfectionist or having a "Type A" personality.

As a reminder, saboteurs are not weaknesses, they are merely a reflection of the behavioral characteristics you were born with. The benefit of the assessment is to increase your self-awareness, becoming more comfortable with yourself and giving yourself options for how you want to proceed. As part of this journey myself, I attended a phenomenal coaching seminar recently, facilitated by Master Certified Coach Sophia Casey, where we learned to "BFF our Saboteurs."

One stickler friend of mine periodically gives herself permission to explore, to discover, to let go. The space she creates with this open-minded approach often leads to epiphanies she never saw coming, and they have shaped her life and career in a direction in line with her soul's purpose. That level of clarity is aspirational, but the beauty of being a stickler is that you can create intentionality out of anything, including letting go, which has given her freedom to relax as a springboard to success, not a guilt-ridden detraction. As I like to say about my own lack of creativity: "I plan my spontaneous time."

Okay, so how can you move forward, knowing you'll never have all the answers?

For me, it was from NFL Hall of Fame Head Coach, Dan Reeves that I first heard about the 80 percent rule. As I sat in the auditorium of our business school, this metric was a powerful unlock for me, providing permission to move forward without 100 percent of what I thought I needed.

Even more aggressive, Jeff Bezos is cited as the originator of the "70 percent rule." Essentially, he says if you have 70 percent of the information needed, make the decision. Sarra Bounouh is a Product leader at Meta who says the 70 percent rule changed her life.[28] Why? Here's her answer:

- Waiting for 90 percent+ information means missed opportunities
- Perfect clarity is often an illusion
- Quick, reversible decisions > slow, perfect ones
- The remaining 30 percent usually comes from actually doing

Bounouh states bluntly, "The cost of inaction is often higher than the cost of a wrong decision."

Wouldn't it be easier to choose a path and stay on that path forever? I wish it were that simple, but it's not. **The expectations for career conviction, clarity, and control are universally elusive.**

Thankfully, you are waking up to the reality of the inevitable twists and turns that come with a career journey. Forbes writer Caroline Castrillon highlights three advantages of a non-linear career path including alignment with your evolving values, growth through diverse experiences, and building resilience through adaptation.[29]

While this may sound challenging, it is true, and I think embracing the benefits of future pivots is a positive step towards embracing change. Acceptance is a lot more powerful than denial.

Kelsey Kubelick, an engineering faculty member at University of Virginia advises, "Students should view uncertainty as an opportunity to gather information through experiences like internships and research. It's normal not to have all the answers at this stage."

Early Experience, Long Term Value

Jon Kropp is the VP of Digital Media at TGL/TMRW Sports (the indoor professional golf league involving Tiger Woods and Rory McIlroy). Jon is a mentor and friend who speaks every year in my Emory University course on Career Navigation. He suggests students envision their career as an hourglass, tilted on its side. As he explains it, at the beginning of your career, all of the sand is on the left side, in the widest part of the container. You can increase your versatility and awareness of the working world by trying a lot of different directions, and along the way you become a generalist—able to adapt to whatever situation comes your way.

Then, over time, the sand enters a more narrow path, based on your interests and your strengths, you become a specialist, knowing more about your thing than anyone else, and that takes you through the heart of your career.

If you are successful enough, you become the manager of a variety of departments or functions and fall back to the generalist point of view. You don't have to be an expert in all of the areas you lead, but you know enough about each one and empower your team to do the rest. You might even come upon a new exploration era that expands your worldview and propels you into another hourglass cycle—an experience I've been fortunate to discover with my new career chapter. In fact, there's much more sand left than I even imagined! :)

26-year-old Garrett has begun finding his way through uncertainty with more confidence. He says,

> *I was obsessed with pursuing a PhD in neuroscience, but have found contentment with my current career path. College helped me identify my skills and interests, leading to a career that combines my passion for research with the ability to make a living. I'm still on a path of slow progression, but I'm now comfortable with the idea of change and transition.*[30]

One of my favorite resources I discovered when writing this book is *The Squiggly Career: Ditch the Ladder, Discover Opportunity, Design Your Career* by Helen Tupper and Sarah Ellis. Just think about the title all by itself, *The Squiggly Career*. This is the norm, not the exception and the authors do an amazing job shedding light on this normalization. Here's one helpful passage:

> *Careers are becoming multi-directional as we move back and forth, in and out of organizations and professions. You don't need to develop every skill simultaneously and at the same pace.* **You can choose what feels most important for you to prioritize at the moment and start taking small steps straight away.**[31]

In the neighborhood of squiggly careers, one of my former co-workers, Kitric Kerns, used AI to design this image that represents his professional journey in the form of a jungle gym.

Career Path Uncertainty | 53

In total, he has spent 33 years in 33 jobs! And guess what—he's successful, happy, and thankful for everything he's experienced. Among the menagerie included these stints:[32]

- Busch Gardens warehouse worker
- TCBY Yogurt (twice)
- Children's Software Producer
- Digital Music Startup Website Producer
- Scuba Diving Instructor (in the Cayman Islands)
- Derivatives Trading Startup Co-Founder
- VP of Product Development
- Venture Studio Co-Founder / Digital Strategist
- Boat Captain

I don't know if your career will have that much variety, but you don't have to worry about that now.

Small steps. Baby steps. One foot in front of the other. Want to take another deep breath? Go ahead. This is a release valve, a chance to take some air out of the stress balloon you are working so hard to keep afloat. **The next time someone asks you what you want to be when you grow up, you have permission to say you're taking it one step at a time,** learning more about yourself and building a variety of skills that will help you adapt to the world around you that continues to evolve.

Remember the question I asked earlier, *What might you want to try next?* Go ahead, take a couple minutes, and jot down some thoughts that come to mind. You're not committing the rest of your life to these ideas, they are merely potential starting points that could evolve into something you never even dreamed was possible. And as you gather more information, you can make a new decision. There's a reason this iconic scene from *Friends* has become a popular career development meme. Pivot!

Career Path Uncertainty | 55

Coaching Question: What's a time you embraced trying something new and it worked out?

CHAPTER 3
Feeling Stuck or Lost

I was in a 'what-am-I-doing-with-my-life' spiral and had to trust the process.

> Jack, 22-year-old recent graduate from the University of Washington[33]

We've all been there. Frozen in time, not sure what to do, what direction to go. No roadmap, no directions, no footprints preceding us on the path to help guide us where to go. Sometimes it's being stuck under a boss that doesn't see you, hear you, or respect you. They're going nowhere and you can't seem to navigate around them. I know you've tried!

In the survey I conducted while writing this book, 64 percent of respondents described themselves as "stuck or lost" regarding their career direction.

Another kind of stuck is being on a career path you don't like, but can't see an escape route. You've already committed time and effort to this pursuit. You chose a major, maybe went to grad school, got the job. And. You. Hate. It. What do you do now?

I remember hitting this wall when I was 26, and it was the catalyst I needed to push me towards business school. More on that situation in the Reality Check chapter later in the book.

One student from Atlanta tried to explain her response to decision fatigue in this way; "I don't know what's going through your mind when you're feeling that stress. For me, it's like a jumble of a bunch of things. My brain is just like, 'Okay, well, we're just not gonna think.'"

I think that feeling has led to what is being called the "NEET" lifestyle. For those who haven't heard of this yet, NEET is an acronym for "Not in Education, Employment, or Training," and describes a growing trend among young people who opt out of traditional career paths. While this may be a conscious choice, it could also reflect a lack of opportunities or difficulties in finding suitable work. This lifestyle can be appealing for its freedom from rigid structures and the potential to pursue personal interests, but it can also lead to social isolation and financial insecurity.[34]

Another trend surfacing is equivalent to a mid-career gap year called "Micro-Retirement." I'll sheepishly admit I first heard about this on the show, *Love Thy Nader*, in which one of the popular sisters quit her job at Deutsche Bank to explore other interests like modeling and entrepreneurship. A *Forbes* article from January 2025 quotes Guy Thornton, the founder of Practice Aptitude Tests, saying Micro-Retirement is a result of, "Younger people prioritizing mental health, personal fulfillment, and meaningful experiences over a singular focus on career longevity and progression."[35]

But what if you feel stuck on a career path your parents nudged (or shoved) you into? It wasn't your desire or your choice. Instead, you're living out *their* dreams, not yours. How do you have that conversation? Will they still love you? They sacrificed to get you this opportunity. Will they be disappointed? How could you walk away from it all?

Okay, that was kind of harsh. My hope is that your parents know you better than anyone else, and they want you to be happy. Having a heartfelt conversation could be more productive than you think. There is more context on family stressors in Chapter 11.

Lost and Found

A few years ago when I started Doyne Career Services, one of my first clients was a former mentee who had since graduated college, gotten her MBA, and had just been laid off from her first job. When we spoke, she kept saying she felt "lost" and didn't know what to do next. My question for her was, **"If you don't want to feel lost, how will you know when you are found?"**

She wasn't alone in her despair. Finding yourself or finding your place in your early twenties is incredibly common and can even be a lifelong search. So instead of yearning for some intangible ideal, I proposed we use a "Found Scale" to measure her progress in the right direction. Session by session, role by role, she continued to experiment and climb the scale and put a puzzle together, a strategy that generated income from a variety of sources, some of which were incredibly fulfilling and on multiple paths that could turn into her dream job. At one point last year, she said to me with a big smile, "I like this new life."

One 19-year-old female college student in Atlanta says she is still feeling off track, "I feel totally lost about what I want to do. Every option seems overwhelming."

In order to address this crisis, Clinical Psychologist Dr. Meg Jay has written a book called *The Defining Decade: Why Your Twenties Matter—And How to Make the Most of Them Now*. Frankly, I think the subtitle is a bit stress-inducing given the implied urgency, but the book contains a lot of truisms, including this quote from one of her clients: "I feel like I'm in the middle of the ocean. Like I could swim in any direction but I can't see land on any side, so I don't know which way to go."[36] Dr. Jay also appeared on an episode of Adam Grant's podcast and discussed one of my favorite chapters—"How to Cook your Way into Confidence and Connection."

As you see yourself at the beginning of this career journey, what are some clues that might be telling you something about where to start? Which direction speaks to you? Can you see how one thing might lead to another? It's impossibly rare to foresee decades down the road, but right now, all you have to do is listen to your heart, analyze with your head, and get moving. There is plenty of time to adjust, adapt and reinvent along the way. You never know what inkling you'll discern, what person you'll encounter, or what lightbulb will go off.

I was at a charity event recently for one of the nonprofits I'm involved with—21st Century Leaders. Every summer, 21CL organizes week-long immersion programs for high school students from across the state of Georgia. During that week, they meet professionals in a variety of industries, exposing them to careers in which they might be interested. I typically join a formal dinner event midweek made up of a few-dozen tables of students who sit with a couple of business folks like me.

The discussions are fascinating, intellectually stimulating, inspiring, and heartwarming. I truly cherish the conversations over those meals and the opportunity to gain more insights about the next generation of all-stars. It always leaves me with immense hope and confidence in our future. I do believe that "children are our future" and our role is to, "teach them well, and let them lead the way." That's my promise to you—I'm here to share what I know and get out of the way.

This past summer, there was a panel discussion that took place towards the end of the 21CL event, moderated by a talented student who is clearly on his way to being a game show or talk show host. Of the distinguished guests on the panel, here is a sampling of their career paths:

- NFL football player turned catering executive
- Lawyer turned political activist
- Accounting student turned CFO of a non-profit
- Journalist turned human resources leader
- A high school dropout from the rough part of Queens who became a major media executive

Take a look at the list above again. We all start somewhere, and it's never exactly where we end up. If you fear your next career decision at the age of 22 could ruin your life, you are going to find out the exact opposite. It's enough to take one step at a time, give it your best shot, and make new decisions when you feel like it's time. You are never truly *stuck*, there is always another direction to go. Remember the compass metaphor?

It's totally understandable to feel this way as you head to college as a wide-eyed teenager on your own for the first time. One freshman female from Michigan who had moved across the country from California says, "I think it's a time where you're really having to learn a lot about yourself. It's the first time for most people, at least for me, without my family. I'm living in a place where I don't know anybody."

A recent engineering grad in Texas mentioned, "It's like I'm stuck at a crossroads—and no direction feels right."

The pressure to know what you're doing also comes from comparison, the feeling of not keeping up with your perception of your peers' pace. "I keep changing my mind about my major and it makes me feel behind everyone else," relayed a 20-year-old female healthcare major in Los Angeles.

Garrett, now 26, echoes this feeling and has gradually made peace with it, "**Being able to separate yourself from somebody else's journey is the ideal goal.** I think that's where you'd find the most success in forging your own career. It's not going to be, like 'hey, my friend did this … I need to do that,' or 'I feel shitty because he's doing this, and I'm doing that.'"

You might also be among the majority of students who prefer to go to Reddit and Chat GPT for advice instead of asking people you know. That finding surprised me at first, but I had to remember that you are part of a generation that grew up as social media natives, with meaningful virtual friendships, and you also lived at home during the COVID-19 pandemic, in relative isolation.

Here's how Cydney, a 24-year-old MBA student in Atlanta, Georgia approaches this inspiration gap: "I like watching interviews of people that I can envision myself, or aspire to, what they're doing. I find that helps a lot because a lot of times I'll hear them in the interviews voice similar sentiments to what I'm feeling now. So it's kind of like, if they were experiencing that, and they're where they're at now, I'm sure I can make it out to where they are."[37]

Sometimes it's an unexpected epiphany that provides clarity. My chiropractor stumbled into his career path when he fell out of a boat during college. He was on a committed path towards dentistry, but when he dislodged a rib, a chiropractor put it back in place, and he decided that's what he wanted to do for the rest of his life.

If you're still not sure how to find a career direction that feels right to you, I've inserted some exercises in the back of this book called *Ikigai* and *FIGure it Out* that my clients of all ages have found helpful.

I realize the last few chapters have been kind of heavy—lots of challenges, real feelings, overwhelming at times. So, now we'll move into some key solutions for stress relief that your peers are finding incredibly helpful.

Coaching Question: Where might you want to be a year from now, and what's one valuable step you can take to move in that direction?

Section 2
Career Stress Solutions

CHAPTER 4
Stress Relief

Spending time with my dog is the best stress relief.

21-year-old female college student, Chicago, Illinois

We have an 11-year-old Goldendoodle named Baxter. About 10 minutes before a storm begins, I know he's getting stressed out because he comes to find me or my wife and gets really close to us—in our office, on the couch, or in the bed. He really hates thunder, and the warning signs are incredibly clear.

People sometimes behave with similar instincts, but don't always have someone to lean on. If you're on your own and sense your anxiety rising, what do you do? Have you already done something or said something you regret before you're able to identify your emotions rising? We all have triggers and relative levels of past trauma that coincide with potentially catastrophic reactivity.

Career-related stress may not be as obvious as described above, and it can sneak up on you. A general malaise can hover over your job until you realize why you aren't feeling great on Monday mornings. But some experiences are more overt—losing out in the final round of interviews, getting ghosted by recruiters, getting an offer revoked the day before you start a new job, or a surprise layoff.

Stress shows up in me as silence, I get quiet or retreat into myself. Or, I lash out and say something mean when I don't intend to be mean. Others crave control, so if you don't have it in one part of your life, you might find yourself straightening magazines on your coffee table or hand towels on the bar of your oven. BTW, I now do this way more than I ever did before. I'm honestly not sure if it's out of love, respect, or that my wife's tendencies were eventually contagious over 27 years of marriage.

Are you able to tell when someone you love is stressed out? What does it look like? Is it a feeling? A gut instinct? Can you just tell? What if looking in a mirror helped you know this feeling about yourself?

I hope you also keep in mind that **not all stress is bad. When channeled, it can provoke action.**

I asked our survey participants about what resources have been most valuable in managing their career-related stress, and responses ranged from family, friends, and pets all the way to mentorship and mental health counseling.[38] See the chart below for additional insights:

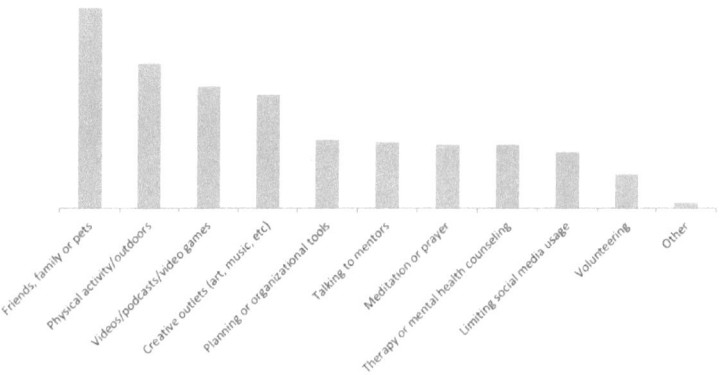

Best resources for managing career-related stress
(among 18-25 year olds)

A key bright spot identified is that recovery is possible. The gap between peak and current stress suggests that stress management, adaptation, or life changes help reduce stress over time. Here are a few hopeful suggestions survey participants wanted to share with their peers:

> *Working out every morning has been the biggest thing for my mood change. I had to find outlets to release stress that I didn't even realize I was feeling.*
> Indiana college student

> *I really just had to take a step back. And I really had to **leave that situation**... reevaluate what I wanted to do, and where I wanted to go in my career.*
>
> 25-year-old male college graduate, Chicago, Illinois

> *You have to tap yourself on the back when you have those little wins.*
>
> 23-year-old female graduate school student, Evanston, Illinois

> *The only thing that helps is **going for a run or being outside**.*
>
> 20-year-old male college student in Miami, Florida.

> *"I **listen to music** to calm down after a stressful day."*
>
> 22-year-old nonbinary design student in San Francisco, California

One of the students I talked to even pointed me towards a Reddit board with a plethora of ideas for overcoming career crisis. I cannot endorse anonymous recommendations, but you're going to look it up anyhow, so here's the link: https://www.reddit.com/r/careerguidance/comments/v1u1kf/how_do_you_overcome_the_quarterlife_career_crisis/

Researcher Dan Buettner wrote *The Blue Zones Solution: Eating and Living Like the World's Healthiest People*. He emphasizes that one of the best ways to reduce stress and lower cortisol levels is to engage in social interaction. This aligns with a core principle of the Blue Zones lifestyle, where strong social networks and community bonds are seen as vital for mental and emotional well-being.

> *Research confirms the significant impact of social connections on health and longevity, with studies showing that strong social relationships can boost the immune system, lower blood pressure, reduce inflammation, and enhance mental health by buffering against depression and anxiety. Loneliness and social isolation, on the other hand, are associated with higher risks of chronic illness and a decreased likelihood of survival.*

In an interview with *Vogue Magazine*, Buettner also says, "One of the best ways to reduce stress—and therefore, cortisol—is just to talk to other people. This can be anyone: a friend, neighbor, colleague, your mom, or the barista."[39]

Maybe, at the end of the day, it's your expectations that need re-setting. John Hartz, the author of *UNworried* says, "Contentment is underrated,"[40] and I think he makes a good point. Do you feel pressure to always look for the next best thing? The better-paying job, the promotion, the next step on the corporate ladder? Ambition is fine, but **if you're always wanting more, when will you ever be happy?**

Mental Health Support

Several interviewees have leaned on therapists for additional support. This is a welcome development, since previous generations were less likely to seek psychiatric consultation.

Says one recent graduate from California, "I have learned to become more open about my stress because that's also something that I struggle with. My friend actually recently said to me, 'I used to think you were not a stressed person at all,' because I'm very good at masking it. I've recently worked on that, because it's just so much better to get it out, because then it's not jumbled up there, at least it's out."

Psychologists like Dr. Mark Cooperberg are also ready to help. Cooperberg is the Director of Psychological Services at Princeton Speech-Language & Learning Center and a Clinical Instructor at Rutgers-RWJ Medical School. His primary work is with children, adolescents, and their families from ages 4 to 40. When I talked to him about his practice, he described his experience as a calling in helping youths with behavioral, emotional, and social difficulties.

Regarding career support, clients often raise challenges with preparing for job interviews and social interactions.[41]

One of the most paradoxical insights I heard was articulated by Alexa, "We are over-connected and feel disconnected at the same time."[42] This leads towards feelings of isolation which exacerbate the pressure felt by many students:

> *I wish colleges talked more about how mental health affects your career. It's not just about grades.*
>
> 22-year-old male engineering graduate in Chicago, Illinois

> *Sometimes I feel like everyone else is coping better than me, but I know that's probably not true.*
>
> 19-year-old nonbinary design major in San Francisco, California

> *I had to take a semester off because my mental health was suffering. It set me back, but I needed it.*
>
> 23-year-old female education graduate in New Orleans, Louisiana

> *Counseling services at my college helped, but I wish there were more sessions available.*
>
> 20-year-old female education major in Boston, Massachusetts

As you can tell, your generation has an evolved relationship with mental health. Cate LeSourd is the author of *Coming of Age: Our Journey into Adulthood*. As a young professional herself, Cate offers this unique perspective, "This younger generation has a little bit more emotional literacy, so they're able to have language for things, they're learning how to communicate emotions." She goes on,

"I've seen that some value their mental health more. They want to experience more of a balanced life, and so I think in that way, they have some coping skills that I don't think my generation did at that age."[43]

In addition to this capacity for talking about stress, more of you see therapy and counseling as a destigmatized option. According to 2022 data from the Substance Abuse and Mental Health Services Administration (SAMHSA), 26.7 percent of 18- to 25-year-olds in the U.S. received mental health treatment in the past year.[44] The American Psychological Association says that more than 37 percent of this age group has received treatment.[45]

Schools like Pacific Oaks College are even increasing licensing programs for therapists as your generation has taken a keen interest in supporting future generations.[46]

Dr. Brandon Smith is known as "The Workplace Therapist." For 20 years he has been committed to improving the health and functioning of people in the workplace. Along the way, he's worn lots of hats: therapist, executive coach, professor, consultant, speaker, radio host, and blogger. For early career professionals, Brandon has introduced the "Workplace Happiness Formula" which is calculated in this way:

Right Job (1 pt.) + Right Culture (1 pt.) + Right Boss (1 pt.) = Workplace Happiness (3 pt. Max)

He suggests that if you are scoring a 1.5 or less, it might be time for a move.[47]

Whether it's in your office, on your college campus, or through your health insurance, access to therapists who are career counselors is readily available. They are knowledgeable, empathetic, and all of your conversations with them are confidential. If you're not ready for an in-person appointment, there are also licensed professionals on TikTok including @drjuliesmith (Dr. Julie Smith), a clinical psychologist who shares educational content on managing anxiety, stress, and burnout—offering practical mental health tools for professionals. You can also look up @nadiaaddesi (Nadia Addesi), a social worker and psychotherapist, who posts about coping with anxiety, self-doubt, and stress in the workplace—focusing on accessible strategies and support. I'm not in a position to explicitly endorse their specific recommendations, but they might just elicit the "aha" you've been looking for.

Dr. David Yeager takes a scientific approach to the mindsets of young adults. He's the Professor of Psychology at the University of Texas at Austin, known for his research on adolescent development, behavior change, and the psychology of motivation. He also wrote the book, 10 to 25: *The Science of Motivating Young People: A Groundbreaking Approach to Leading the Next Generation—And Making Your Own Life Easier.*

Insights abound in Yeager's work, including this thought, "Although stressful experiences feel unpleasant in the moment, they are the path through which everyone who ever became really good at something got to where they are."[48] He also points out the changing perceptions of stress. Rather than viewing stress as inherently harmful, it can be reframed as a natural and even beneficial part of growth and achievement. This shift in perspective can significantly impact how you approach challenges and perform under pressure.

If you're a few years into your career, you might think it makes the most sense to continue climbing the ladder in a vertical direction. I would never judge you for chasing dollars, but one strategic angle to consider is making a lateral move to a different role or department. You might not increase your compensation immediately, but you can expand your skillset and long-term marketability.

You can also develop new relationships which will help you build "personal capital"—one of the most valuable assets you will bring to the table over the course of your career. Of course, learning what isn't for you is just as important and valuable as what is for you.

Here are a few more thoughts from twenty-somethings. Which stress relief option do you think is worth trying next?

> *I'm a big reader, and finding time to put that into the schedule is really important for me.*
>> Alexa, 22-year-old female journalism graduate in California.

> *I manage stress by being very proactive. It's talking to people. It's reaching out. It's networking, it's applying to things when you don't want to, and*

you'd rather just sit on your bed and hang out with your friends.
Caydence, 20-year-old college student in
Ann Arbor, Michigan[49]

Don't be so hard on yourself. I think that's really hard to do, but you have to give yourself grace.
Simone, 22-year-old graduate student in Illinois[50]

And, if you had your wish granted, you'd like to have greater access to the resources ranked in the chart below.[51] We'll be touching on most of these in the next few chapters.

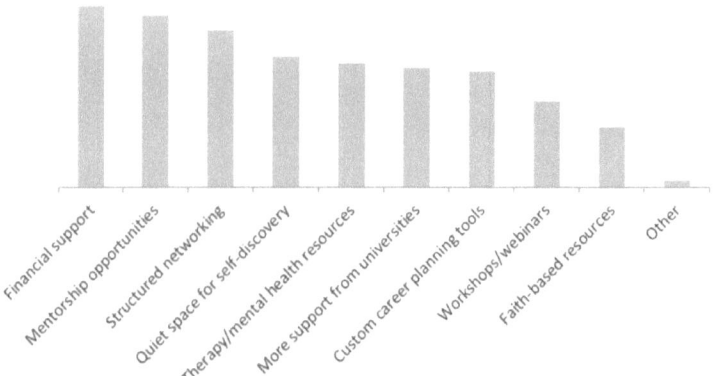

Coaching Question: What's something you did in the last year that helped reduce your stress?

CHAPTER 5
Mentoring

I don't have a mentor. I've never had a mentor.
Cydney, 24-year-old female MBA student, Atlanta, Georgia

Mentors have been credited by many as pivotal to career clarity and growth. From the research I conducted for this book, 63 percent of respondents credited a mentor or teacher with helping them clarify their career path. 72 percent expressed interest in adult transition workshops that include mentorship. Reddit was specifically cited as a primary source of mentorship in one interview.

For those of you who haven't been fortunate enough to have mentors helping you guide your career, here are some quotes from students who have seen them make a big impact:

> *My mentor helped me see possibilities I never considered.*
> 21-year-old female college graduate, San Francisco, California

> *Mentors and advisors really changed my perspective on life and career.*
> 22-year-old male college graduate, California

> *I've learned personal strategies for managing stress, including listening to music and focusing on controllable aspects of life, from a mentor.*
> Tristin, 25-year-old male entrepreneur[52]

> *One (resource) that has been most helpful are organized mentorship programs where people are assigned to you. If you put the work in, you get the most return on investment because they want to talk to you.*
> Caydence, Michigan college sophomore

With that said, many of you still yearn for the opportunity:

> *I've never had a mentor, and I think that's why I feel so lost.*
> 22-year-old nonbinary college student, Portland, Oregon

Mentorship is the one thing I wish my school emphasized more.
23-year-old male, Atlanta, Georgia

Before I knew about professional coaching, mentoring was my Valhalla—a calling of sorts, it came so naturally. I'm sure part of it is the ego benefit—others looking up to me with an air of respect that most of us crave deep down inside. The first experience I ever had as a mentor was in high school when I became a "Big Brother" to a troubled young elementary school student who had a rough home life and no male role model. As I was only 16 at the time, it was pretty eye opening, and humbling. I was part of a middle-to-upper class family with two wonderful parents and a generally safe and privileged existence. He did not have any of those advantages, and the rate at which he gravitated towards me was a shock to my system, almost scary that he looked up to me so much, and so quickly. We went bowling, went out to eat a couple of times, and I stopped by his home occasionally to check on him. I'll admit, I was getting attached to him, too. It feels good to be admired, wanted, and needed. As I reflect on that special connection, it feels like the fuel for many of my subsequent mentoring and managing relationships. It's why I say that I may seem selfless at times, but it's also selfish.

My Mentoring Lightbulb Moment

In 2011, I was running part of the National Basketball Association (NBA) digital business, which essentially included P&L responsibilities for NBA.com. It was a great job with talented people, and we were doing really well as a business and helping the growth of the league overall. Then, a work stoppage happened, lasting 161 days, from July 1 to December 8, triggered by a failure to agree on a new collective bargaining agreement (CBA). It was a tough time for a lot of people, including those of us responsible for producing content and experiences for NBA fans. The fans were pissed, and we had to completely reconfigure NBA.com to eliminate player imagery. We found a creative outlet by building out historical content, but it was generally a slow and unfulfilling slog.

One of those days that fall, I noticed I felt better at the end of the day. So I asked myself "why?". Upon reflection, I realized I had talked to one of my mentors that day and talked to a mentee, as well. That light bulb meant so much to me because I had identified a key element in my happiness—the give-and-take of mentoring relationships. From that week forward, I intentionally scheduled mentoring sessions every Friday—pretty much for the rest of my career—and of course, I'm still continuing it today in my coaching practice.

I remember hanging out with a friend of mine in the neighborhood about five years ago, and we were talking about our careers. Offhandedly, I mentioned something about "my mentees," and he kind of looked at me weirdly and asked, "mentees?" This wasn't that long ago, so it wasn't strange to me that an executive would have a bunch of younger employees whom he helps out. At that moment, I realized that it was special. It was actually a gift. Something others aren't as inclined towards.

I'm not saying I'm special. I'm saying this is something I was doing organically that others were not. It's a strange thing about strengths that I've come to understand. Certain skills that come easily to us we don't readily define as strengths, because they don't inherently require concerted effort. It's just stuff we do. And it's not until you realize the relative nature of those skills compared to others that it stands out as a strength.

It's also important that there's representation of people who look like you in the careers you hope to pursue. As has been said, "If you see it, you can be it." One of my former bosses said that when she used to be a guest lecturer at Emory Law School, a lot more female students would come up to her after class or during office hours, than her male colleagues.

President Barack Obama addressed this in his Barnard College commencement speech from 2012, "Until a girl can imagine herself, can picture herself, as a computer programmer, or a combatant commander, she won't become one. Until there are women who tell her, 'Ignore our pop culture obsession over beauty and fashion and focus instead on studying and inventing and competing and leading,' she'll think those are the only things that girls are supposed to care about."[53]

Dr. Stacey Young Rivers, author of *Career Smarts for College Students*, says, "**Having a mentor is like downloading the game codes to the next level**. Getting access unlocks a wealth of knowledge." It's also not just a one-way street, she continues, "Reverse mentoring often occurs as part of the reciprocity of the relationship, and each person walks away richer as a result."[54]

Finding a Mentor

If you're looking for a mentor, you might be wondering how to find one, or how to ask someone, right? Here's a starting point ... do you remember when you needed reference letters for your college applications? You had to go to one of your teachers, or a sports coach, club sponsor, or summer camp supervisor for a statement that supported your candidacy. You might have also done this when you applied to jobs. References are a great starting point to consider for possible mentors. If you've already had a few jobs, former managers also might be excellent mentors, if they remember you fondly (and vice versa). It doesn't need to be a formal request, but you can ask them if it's okay if you reach out in the future as your career develops. I've met with some of my mentees on a quarterly basis for the last 15 years!

Parul Khosla is the CEO of Arena, an AI-powered career platform that just launched a new feature called Pow-

Mentoring | 85

erMatch. She says, "It's hard to ask people to find their own mentors when they're so early in their career. I think things that young people can do to find mentorship is to ask managers or people that you work with that are low-lifts. They already know you in some sense, and they want to help you." She also says it can be a more informal relationship, "You don't have to say 'Hey, can you be my mentor?' But, you can say 'I want to learn more from you about your career, and maybe we could sit down once a month and just talk through my career.'"[55]

One recent graduate from Indiana mentioned college professors as a great option for mentorship. In her case, "Those were people that understand what jobs exist. They all have experience of getting their first job."

Kelsey, a faculty member at the University of Virginia agrees, saying academic advisors, industry speakers, and alumni networks can provide valuable connections for students. "We have a seminar series with different people coming in from industry or academia, and there will be opportunities for students to interact with that person more in a small group capacity. Alums of the program are fans of the university, right? Great people to be able to talk to. So I think that's a really nice resource."

I hope this helps you feel less alone on your journey. On that team effort, here's an excerpt from *Designing your Life*, by Bill Burnett and Dave Evans:

"Life design is intrinsically a communal effort. When you are wayfinding a step or two at a time to build (not solve)

your way forward, the process has to rely on the contribution and participation of others. Finding someone who can give you good counsel and who regularly leaves you in a clearer and more settled state of mind is a great asset. This is where good mentors shine."[56]

Specific mentoring programs also exist, and you might fit their criteria for applying:

- **Introships** is a nonprofit internship program that evolved from in-person to online during COVID-19, eventually leading to the development of a career coaching component. It is essentially a career discovery program for college students, modeled after design thinking, which includes individual testing, video or Zoom calls, and coaching. The program has scholarships available for those who cannot afford it. Joe Fiveash, the founder, even noted that presenters are open to networking with the students, and often have mentoring conversations.

- **Project Wall Street** is a nonprofit workforce readiness program, providing professional development and executive-quality coaching services to underprivileged, first-generation students interested in careers in finance. Founder Jordan Burick is the CEO and a financial literacy advocate.

- The **American Marketing Association** in Atlanta has a formal mentoring initiative, open to all members, and I have participated myself. The program offers marketers the opportunity to network, gain new skills, and develop lasting relationships with each other. By connecting like-minded professionals through the matching process, the AMA makes building connections effortless, so all young professionals need to do is show up, ready to grow.

My first official mentor was part of a formal program while I was in business school. I was fortunate to be paired with Edward Rosenfeld, an alumnus who worked in the media industry, my chosen field. One of the first events I attended with Edward was to see one of the richest people in the world, Warren Buffett, speak at a massive gathering in Glenn Memorial Church, which was larger than any auditorium on campus. When Buffett began his speech, he tapped the microphone in front of him and said, "Testing, testing, one billion, two billion, three billion." I still laugh about it today. Some people operate on a different level.

Anyhow, Edward has provided priceless guidance over the years, not the least of which was at the very beginning of our relationship. He asked me what kind of job I was looking for. At that point, I didn't know much about the business world—it seemed like the only two options were marketing and finance, and I wasn't going into finance. So I said marketing, and he gave me a homework assignment to look at all of the job descriptions I could find to determine what kind of marketing roles most appealed to me.

Through that process, I gained conviction that I was most interested in the strategic/analytical side of the function, and not so much advertising or branding. Even that one boost of clarity helped me make some decisions about which courses to take and which professors I would try to spend more time with.

Later in my career, I was able to turn the tables and take on a mentorship role, paying it forward from the support I had been given over the years.

As a token of my gratitude, I'd like to thank a few people for showing me the path that led to my newest calling in coaching through mentoring: Betsy Holland, Sydney Langdon, Valerie Immele, and Dawn Simonton. You all invited me to be part of mentoring programs where I was able to find myself, develop as a leader, and discover the joy of helping others help themselves.

Coaching Question: Who is someone in your life who could be a valuable mentor?

CHAPTER 6
Networking

"I wish someone would show me how to network. It seems like everyone else already knows."

Male, 20-year-old college student,
Phoenix, Arizona

Where do I begin? I love networking. I love connecting with people, hearing their stories, discovering things in common, helping each other. Nothing happens without reaching out. Sure, I've had plenty of situations that were uncomfortable, and I still do. Cocktail parties where I don't know anyone. Fancy work events with executives who seem beyond me. I have found myself tongue-tied many times, including my first chance meeting with NBA Commissioner Adam Silver at the 2010 NBA All-Star Technology Summit Reception in Orlando. Fortunately, I had a chance to meet him with better results a few years later, once I got my words together.

Based on the research for this book, I don't need to convince you of the value of networking.

Here are a few more soundbites to get the motivation flowing ...

> *The best opportunities I've found came from talking to people, not job boards.*
> 24-year-old female college graduate in Chicago, Illinois

> *Having a good network is life-changing; connections open doors.*
> Jack, 22-year-old University of Washington graduate

> *LinkedIn and connections have been huge for me; it's about putting in the work.*
> Max, 22-year-old college graduate from California

> *I have gotten all of my progress in my career from networking.*
> Alexa, 22-year-old college graduate in California

In terms of career pursuit, (the greatest value) will always be ... the network.
>William, 26-year-old engineering graduate in Atlanta, Georgia

My First Conference

I remember going to my first industry conference in the fall of 2001. I was a naive MBA student at Goizueta Business School and determined to break into the media industry at a new level. I had been on the production side of the business previously, but that didn't come with formal networking opportunities. It began with an idea among a few of us that we would get involved in a local Atlanta chapter of CTAM—the Cable Telecommunications Association of Marketing. As the corporate home of Turner Broadcasting, CNN, Cox Communications, and The Weather Channel, there was a decent amount of activity in Atlanta, which, of course, paled compared to NY, LA, and even Chicago at some level.

Nevertheless, following the 1996 Atlanta Olympics, it became a southeastern hub for other media companies that wanted sales teams spread around the country. The local CTAM board included members of the locally based organizations, and also delegates from media powerhouses like MTV Networks, Scripps, Discovery, and a fledgling version of Comcast, which had been ATT Broadband at the time.

With enough initiative, my colleagues and I navigated our way into a local happy hour as the "young professionals" delegation. I have a few pictures of that event at a wine bar in Buckhead. First of all, I can't believe how young we look. Secondly, that took some chutzpah! I can't explain how we overcame our trepidation except to say that ignorance is bliss.

With a decent "showing" at that event, I was invited to the national CTAM conference in Boston later that year. I do remember being nervous at some level, but I was also a kid in a candy store. Totally in awe. The keys to the castle. I was on my way! There were dinners and drinks and panels and handshakes. I even got to meet Mark Cuban! This was pre-Shark Tank—he was CEO of HDNet at the time. My friend says I talked to him for 30 seconds, none of which I remember.

As an MBA student, I had my sights set on post-graduation employment, so I had a list of people I wanted to talk to while I was there—ideally Atlanta contacts, as that was becoming a comfortable home for Aimee and me. But I was also open to all of it. Come what may, get in the mix, see what happens. I still recall a few of the Turner and Cox folks that I was "targeting" at the time, and some I even got to work with eventually.

Did my appearance at the conference have something to do with that? Not really, but it did open my eyes to the possibilities and was the first time I could really see myself as a business person in that setting. Maybe that's what propelled my willingness and interest in networking. The more you do, the more it's addictive. I can visualize the atoms colliding, forming new bonds, building relationships, staying in touch over so many years. The proof is in the outcomes and it all started with a dream and a little courage to put myself out there.

Let's go back a little further ... what else could have emboldened my mojo that you could also experience? I did have high school leadership opportunities—team captain, president of a couple of clubs. Was it an advantage that when I was only 13 years old I spoke on stage in front of all of my friends and family at my Bar Mitzvah? I didn't really have a business-minded role model to follow. My dad was certainly social when I saw him at his office schmoozing patients and parents. But the stories I hear of my grandfathers who were in clothing sales and media, respectively, might be the genetic clues to my predisposition.

Last fall, I was invited to be part of a networking event for student athletes at Emory University. I do a lot of work at Emory and volunteer in various ways. Given my sports background, I've worked with a lot of former college and pro athletes and they're some of the best clients and mentees I've ever had—disciplined, accountable, driven, and coachable. At that event, with several sports executives in attendance, some of the students were reluctant to talk at first. Those who readily engaged really stood out and got a ton of value from the event, gathering contact information which led to valuable industry introductions.

As you might have realized, **most people born after 2000 have difficulties with in-person communication**. Feeling "socially awkward" is totally normal. As a starting point, you've grown up with social media and virtual relationships as the norm. Then, the COVID-19 pandemic kept many of you secluded in your homes and bedrooms during your formative teenage years. The impact of that era will be studied for years and remain a question that every therapist asks their clients: "What was going on in your life in 2020, and how did that isolation affect you?"

Yes, You Can

With that said, I've developed a networking methodology that seems to break young professionals out of their fearful shells. It's called ICAN, and stands for: Identify, Connect, Ask, and Navigate.

Identify - Who do you want to contact?

Connect - What do you have in common?

Ask - Be Specific—What do you want?

Navigate - Follow Up—Who else might they know?

Try this exercise with a practical situation. Is there a company you want to work for? Is there a client you're trying to attract? Experiment with a variety of connection messages, and ask to see what works best. If you shoot enough shots using this strategic framework, you'll increase your engagements and conversions.

The purpose of this ICAN framework is to break the process down into a series of gamified steps that lead to disassociation and trial. It becomes a step-by-step approach that gets people out of their heads and developing some momentum towards that addictive serum I mentioned previously. Once they get the ball rolling, they see the power of proactivity. You can't expect a 100 percent response rate, but as this metaphor follows the baseball world: If you get 3 hits out of 10 at bats, you're in the Hall of Fame!

One of my clients began our partnership as a relatively shy recent graduate trying to land her first job out of college. After getting to know each other and building some trust, we used the ICAN framework for a practical situation—she was trying to make contact with a local company in her industry of interest. She was bold enough to play the game, tried out a few different networking messages on LinkedIn, and successfully scheduled a few informational interviews. A few months later, I'm proud to say, she has gained a ton of confidence—reaching out to people on her own, and she landed a great job in the process. More on LinkedIn in Chapter 9 regarding leveraging social media.

One concept that I've seen proven true in action is called **"weak ties,"** as referenced by Dr. Meg Jay in *The Defining Decade*. She explains that the power of weak ties lies in expanding opportunities—"It is the people we hardly know, and not our closest friends, who will improve our lives most dramatically."

The way I see this visually is like a bullseye target. Your core relationships are in the center circle—friends, family, colleagues, managers, teachers, etc. Those are strong ties, the people you know directly. The second circle beyond that is your weak ties. The people that your strong ties know, but you don't. The beauty of this double layered approach is that you can be totally honest with your strong ties—tell them what you're looking for, what company you want to work for, what contact you'd like to be introduced to. At that point, an introduction is an implied endorsement, and it's highly targeted to the people who can impact your situation.

I know this may be tough for you. Jonathan Haidt, author of *The Anxious Generation*, put it bluntly as he spoke about his book on the "Armchair Experts" podcast, "Technology has decimated human interaction."[57] Getting your generation comfortable with contacting professionals is complicated. You've grown up with social media, and there's some progress you can make building relationships through social media, but it's more important to look people in the eye, shake their hand, and know how to ask questions in person.

When Jordan Burick was trying to get a Wall Street investment banking job, he engineered a networking event for himself where he was the only candidate. He set it all up from Greensboro, North Carolina, without a flight or a hotel and once he confirmed enough coffee chats, he booked the cheapest travel arrangements possible and successfully created his own Super Day.[58]

Finding a way to get my younger clients more comfortable with networking has taught me a lot about not telling people to be somebody different than themselves. I think there's a natural way to build relationships without being a self-promoting braggart. There are ways to do it. I've developed another methodology where people who are more on the introverted side of the socialization scale can **approach networking as a research project.** When you're trying to learn something about your intended industry or target company, you can take it step-by-step where you convert your resistance into curiosity.

That's the light bulb I want to turn on. I'm not going to write your messages for you. I'm not telling you, "Here's who to reach out to—go do it!" It's about providing the tools, the confidence, the capacity, and the motivation to go about things interpersonally, because it's going to pay a very long-term dividend that you're not even aware of yet. Sometimes it's just about finding something in common and creating a simple connection.

Here's a networking suggestion that sounds like a good starting point, from Olaoluwa Oguneye, a 19-year-old who I met previously through the 21st Century Leaders program:

> *I'm about to let you in on one of the best ways I've found to build real, lasting connections with people. Find a*

hobby. Or reconnect with one you used to love. Then go out and find community around it.

For me, it's basketball. And through pickup runs, I've ended up building friendships with everyone from the head of content at MrBeast, to quants at Citadel and Optiver, to startup founders shaping the next wave of tech, all just by showing up and hooping. (And this is just in 2025)

When you're doing something you genuinely enjoy, connection happens naturally. The pressure of "networking" fades. You're not trying to impress anyone, you're just being yourself. And that's when the most meaningful connections tend to form.

So here's a challenge: pick up something new this month. Or dust off something you haven't touched in a while. And don't do it alone, find others who love it, too. You never know who you'll meet, or how far it'll take you.[59]

Coaching Question: What professor could introduce you to alumni in your targeted field?

Section 3

The Job Search

CHAPTER 7
Finding a Job/ Internship

It feels like every job wants experience I don't have.

22-year-old female college graduate,
New York, New York

Did somebody change the rules of the game? Yep. If that's how you're feeling, you're absolutely right. Whatever happened to the promise of getting a degree in a particular major that leads directly to a job? I'm not saying the linear career path is completely extinct, but it's on life support.

You still need a doctorate degree and/or board-certified license for several professions—medical, legal, etc. However, much of what remains is in doubt.

In fact, for the first time in recorded US economic history, **the unemployment rate for recent college graduates is worse than the national average.**[60] As reported by The Bureau of Labor, "Employment in technology fields across all sectors fell by around 214,000 jobs in April 2025, according to tech trade association CompTIA."[61]

One interviewee explains her predicament in this difficult market by saying, "The job market obviously adds a lot of stress to it, just because it's so stringent and it's just really, really difficult to get a job, not to mention a job that you organically enjoy."

Do any of these sentiments sound familiar?

> *I've applied to 50 internships and heard back from two.*
> 21-year-old male college student, Chicago, Illinois

> *The process is so discouraging—I almost want to give up.*
> 23-year-old female college graduate, New Orleans, Louisiana

> *The job market isn't what I expected. It's a wake-up call.*
> 25-year-old male college graduate, New York, New York

Finding a Job/Internship | 103

I completely blew an interview last week, and don't know what to do next.
22-year-old female college graduate,
Fort Mill, South Carolina

A recent CNBC report found that 57 percent of rising seniors (class of 2025) already felt negatively about the job market going into their senior year, according to a study from Handshake.[62] Job creation has slowed significantly and this graduating class is applying to more jobs than in past years to increase their odds.[63]

LinkedIn executive, Aneesh Raman, echoes these concerns in a *New York Times* article entitled, "I See the Bottom Rung of the Career Ladder Breaking."[64] Among his takeaways, he cites the following statistics:

- The unemployment rate for college grads has risen 30 percent since September 2022, compared with about 18 percent for all workers.[65]
- Members of Generation Z are more pessimistic about their futures than any other age group out there.[66]

Raman continues to say we should, "redesign first jobs with growth in mind—roles that teach adaptability, not repetition, and serve as springboards, not stalls." I think this hits the nail on the head for what you are looking for—**opportunity**. Entry level work is in the process of changing forever as a result of AI and technological advances in general. White collar office work will be delegated to machines which means you have an opportunity to skip a rung of the traditional job ladder. Are you ready for it?

This is a challenge that can be wrapped into the concept of "adulting." You will need to "grow up" in the eyes of your employer if you want to make a positive impression and immediate contribution, and the resulting path can lead to faster promotions and earning potential, judged more by measurable meritocracy than ever before. Accomplishing this is not far from your reach. I've met plenty of you and you're honestly more mature than plenty of adults I've worked with. However, there are some life skills that still concern you in a way that betrays your age.

I talked to a college junior recently who is double majoring in computer science and analytics, and she has a return internship offer to a Fortune 500 company following her first summer with them. Even she is stressing out over having a job at graduation. I'm not saying you shouldn't have some concern about entry level opportunities, but if you're doing all you can do to put yourself in a good position, your biggest challenge might be how you are managing your anxiety.

I promise you that all hope is not lost. There are reasons for optimism. For example:

- Technological advancements have lowered barriers to entry in many fields
- Social media has enabled the influencer generation
- A smoother path to entrepreneurship has created career flexibility

- Ride-sharing and e-commerce have unlocked the gig economy
- The Health Tech and FinTech industries are currently growing at extraordinary rates

Certainly, the proliferation of Artificial Intelligence can be considered a threat to entry level employment, but it can also be your greatest advantage. More on that in Chapter 10.

When I think about my kids, students, and young coaching clients, I also want them to make the most of their time on campus, as it's more fleeting than you realize.

While you're in college, aren't you supposed to have time for some fun? One student responded to the survey this way, "You're expected to go get a job, but you don't know how to do it. You're expected to also simultaneously enjoy being a student, while trying not to worry about things in the future."

In 1996, the year I graduated from college, I remember job searching on Monster.com, the ancient predecessor to Indeed. This was the very early days of the World Wide Web, so the only jobs listed online were for software engineers and vaunted "webmasters." It was natural that the early adopters of the internet would be more tech-savvy than most and therefore create their own marketplace. Self-serving? Absolutely.

Gradually that online job market expanded to become what you see today on LinkedIn or Zip Recruiter (apologies to Career Builder and HotJobs for flying past an entire era of job-finding websites). I didn't find anything very interesting for several months and ended up taking a part-time job with a financial services company—cold calling and mailing letters to prospective clients. While the job itself was pretty boring, I did get some of the best investment education of my life.

In this way, every job has the potential for long term value. You might learn some of your best skills like multi-tasking or communication from working in retail or restaurant jobs. My son's college bartending gig opened him up to an entirely new world of professional options that leverage his newly identified relationship-building skills.

The current state of affairs for job seekers is really a self-guided tour with twists and turns around every corner. Do you ever feel like you're being swallowed up by quicksand or the rug is constantly being pulled out from under you?

I wish I could tell you that stability is the norm. It's not. The situation is challenging. According to the National Association of Colleges and Employers (NACE), "employers extended fewer offers of full-time employment to their 2023-2024 interns than in the past. The average rate — 62% — was the lowest in more than five years."[67]

You will need to be nimble, adaptable, and resilient. I'm sorry if that's not the message you wanted to hear, but it's the truth. The good news is that you can be all of those things, but you might need to reset your expectations and train for a long-haul journey. Instead of turn-by-turn instructions from your favorite mapping app, **can you**

Finding a Job/Internship | 107

think of your career trajectory more as a compass? Are you heading in the right general direction? If not, can you make slight adjustments to your course? What steps can you take to be more prepared for change? Can you find a way to be at peace with your current situation?

Internship programs exist in a lot of companies across a variety of industries. Of course, not every opportunity is a Google, McKinsey or Nvidia, but you might find some "under the radar" roles that are less competitive and still right for you:

- Many public sector internships are listed at USA-Jobs.gov.
- Idealist.com is one hiring home of non-profit and volunteer organizations, currently listing 50+ paid internships
- For college students looking for commercial real estate opportunities, the Urban Land Institute offers courses and programs that prepare you for the workforce.[68]
- Interested in Science? Check out career websites for museums like the Smithsonian or those in your own state.

If you want to pursue a path that punches you in the face with constant rejection, try the entertainment industry, or in my case, the sports business. Rejection sucks, but getting a job in one of these industries is extremely hard, so rejection is going to be part of the process. There are so many people interested, and only so many jobs. There's no formal recruiting process, there are a lot of unpaid internships, and with diligent networking, anything is possible.

In the book, *What Does Your Fortune Cookie Say?* by Adam Albrecht, there's an entertaining list of 80 life lessons grounded in positive thinking. Trust me when I tell you that Adam has the energy of a 20-year-old, although he's actually more than twice that age. Among the morsels he dishes out, I found Chapter Eight especially tasty: "The person with the most keys will open the most doors." The "Last Bite" of that chapter goes on to say:

> *There are keys to unlocking problems everywhere. Find them in the things you read and the experts you meet. Discover them through experience and observation. So look for them. Collect them before you need them. And be prepared for whatever your world and your work send your way.*[69]

I know it's daunting, but I have to agree with Adam—control what you can control by taking specific actions that might open the right door at the right time. For me, the most productive path was a series of internships that led me to the (un)promised land.

Once upon a time, I was an intern. Actually, many times. Here's a quick trip down memory lane that illuminates a few impactful internships in my career, along with some lessons learned and questions for you to ponder.

PASS Sports Television
Summer between Sophomore and Junior Year

What it was: Unpaid Production Assistant internship covering 50 Detroit Tigers games for a regional sports network.

How I got it: Applied via mail (before email was widely used). Brought a highlight tape to the interview with a Michigan sports montage edited over the sound of The Victors fight song. I was hired by Jim Holly and also mentored by Ed Kaltz, who occasionally spoiled me with a Detroit Coney dog.

How it went: The Tigers lost 84 games that season, and I officially broke into the business, doing everything I could to help the production crew. Despite the ridiculous afro I sported at the time, I must have made a decent impression because it led directly to paid freelance gigs on football and hockey broadcasts.

Bad break/Bright side: I drove roundtrip 86 miles per game and wasn't reimbursed for mileage, parking, or meals. I realize this is a choice that not everyone can afford, which is why I am a firm advocate for paid internships.

Lessons Learned: Always bring something special to the interview.

Question for Applicants: What internship will best set you up for your next step?

CNN
Summer during Business School

What it was: Unpaid Business Operations internship in the CNN News Group.

How I got it: The sister-in-law (Tamara Schwartz) of a business school classmate (Michael Schwartz) introduced me to the hiring managers (Scott Williams, Mike Zarrilli, and Jay Higginbotham).

How it went: Great group of managers who had me analyze a mountain of expense data to formulate cost savings recommendations. I also helped develop the first-ever CNN Mobile marketing strategy. While I was there, I met as many MBAs and Emory alumni across Turner as I could.

Bad break/Bright side: I didn't get paid for this internship, so I decided to spend every Friday working on my first startup venture—a purse business!

Lessons Learned: Networking works. Great managers matter. **If a door opens, explore the whole house.**

Question for Applicants: Who do you know that knows someone you want to know? Who else?

NASCAR.COM
Final semester of Business School

What it was: My first paid internship ($15/hour!). I was hired to help with strategy and analysis for a NASCAR digital subscription product within the company known at that time as AOL Time Warner.

How I got it: Stacey Rudnick in the Goizueta Business School career office knew the hiring manager, Lee Bushkell, and helped me get an interview. My experience with an extracurricular consulting project for *TV Guide* online was the relevant industry knowledge that I believe clinched the offer. Amazingly, that was the only official interview I had in my 20 year tenure with Turner Sports.

How it went: More great managers and lucky timing with the growth of sustainable internet business models.

Bad break/Bright side: At the end of one year, the internship ended without a full-time offer. The next week, our son was born, and the week after that, I was hired with benefits! Many thanks to Lee and the Turner Sports Interactive legends, including Jon Kropp, Michael Adamson, Scott Bailey, and Drew Reifenberger. I'll be forever grateful for the opportunity.

Lesson Learned: School projects can help you land jobs.

Question for Applicants: What area of the company has the greatest growth possibilities?

When I was graduating from college, and again after business school, I got a lot of job rejections. While frustrated, I wasn't deterred. There's a fine line between stubbornness and persistence. I also had the support of my family—for which I have been very grateful. And frankly, I had financial advantages that allowed me to pursue a path I was passionate about.

In the end, I completed 25 years in the sports industry and have now made it a full-time mission to help others define and achieve their dreams. As a career coach, I'm now talking to several people every day who are working hard to land their next role. It's a very tough market, and it's hard to watch them endure their struggles, but I'm an eternal optimist, and I do believe you can prepare yourself to be lucky.

If you're finding yourself struggling through this process, and suffering from the mental toll of rejection and ghosting, I'd like you to channel this question posed by one of my interviewees: *"What is your relationship with your job search?"* I know it can feel all-consuming and hopeless at times, but it's imperative to prioritize your mental and physical health as part of the process. It's not time away from applying and networking that should make you feel guilty. It's quite the opposite, as will be shared in later chapters, stress management is a critical part of the process that leads to a fulfilling career path.

Alternate Approaches to Getting Experience

One other option for getting experience before you have experience is in class, as endorsed by technology executive and author Dr. Stacey Young Rivers. She says, "School projects offer more than just grades; they provide a platform to showcase your skills and creativity."

Instead of asking about a formal internship, you can also ask prospective employers, *"Can I help you with a project?"* Everyone has a project they can't get to because they're too busy.

Joining the military is another option many have pursued that paid off financially and also provided transferable skills they employed in the workforce once they completed their service. Former active-duty Army officer Harman Lindsey has been able to parley his talents into the video game industry and says that in the military, "You get a breadth of work experience that is unparalleled."

North American Trade Schools points towards another path to gainful employment, noting "careers in construction, welding, electrical work, HVAC, commercial truck driving, and diesel technology are experiencing rapid growth in 2025."

Since its founding in 2015, a company named Parker Dewey has been at the forefront of connecting employers with the next generation of talent through short-term, professional assignments they call micro-internships.[70] I love this kind of approach that creates bite-sized experiences for all young professionals to get experience and learn more about what you want from your career.

I truly hope you don't give up. I have many clients who have gone through the same exhausting process as you, and they're eventually finding their way to a great beginning. After interviewing with seven different companies and coming up short, one client I talked to just moved into her Charlotte, North Carolina, apartment after landing an entry level job in her chosen field. Another client secured a post-graduate internship at a sports agency and continues to make connections that will pay off long into the future. A third client patiently waited for her entertainment internship to eventually turn into a part-time job and then develop into a full-time job with benefits. **Success is absolutely possible, but it does require persistence, hard work, and patience.**

Coaching Question: What creative approach can you take to gain experience in your target industry?

CHAPTER 8
College Career Resources

I didn't even know we had a career office until senior year.
21-year-old education major, Cleveland, Ohio

I'm going to lay this out here up front—**something is not working between students and their college career centers.** Before my inbox overflows with angry emails from university career advisors, I know it isn't a universal problem. Your school may be helping students in extraordinary ways. But, during the process of writing this book, almost everything I heard from 18- to 25-year-olds about the assistance they received from their college career center has been problematic. If you are one of the students who has an exceptional advisor running an impactful program, then please let me know: What's their secret? What are they doing to connect with you? How are they making it work? I promise I will share some bright spots before this chapter concludes.

Going back to the survey, when I asked students what career resources they have used most often, they led with family and the internet. Their college's Career Office ranked 9th.[71]

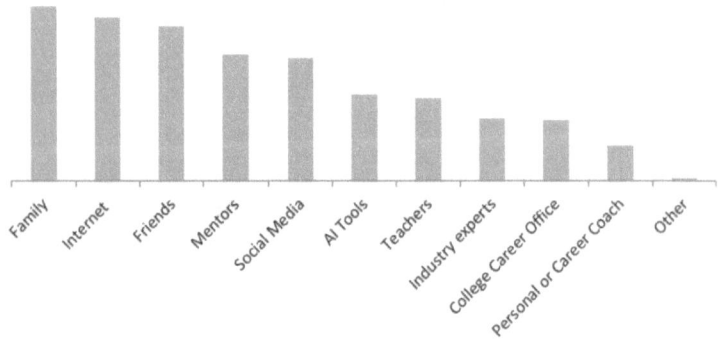

Here is a data point I can't turn away from: 60 percent of students are unaware of the services offered at their institutions.[72] Just as troubling, 31 percent of students surveyed say they haven't interacted with their campus career center at all.[73]

What's going on? Here are a couple of quotes for some added context:

> The Career Development Center didn't support me in my specific career. So we have career fairs. That has been really helpful for certain people. But for me, I walked around a career fair and never saw a job that really caught my attention. I had a plan or an idea, and none of those really fit.
>
> 20 year-old female sophomore college student

> "Universities should place more emphasis on job preparation, like designing courses or requiring workshops rather than placing the emphasis on success in courses that won't matter. I feel like a lot is said about it, but not a lot is actually done or required of students to make us feel more prepared.
>
> 21 year-old female college graduate, San Francisco, California

It's not all doom and gloom, but students are looking for enhanced support: *"The career center is helpful, but I wish they had more industry connections,"* says a 23-year-old engineering graduate in Boston, Massachusetts.

Success does happen, as with a female 22-year-old business major in Chicago, "My college career office helped me land my first internship."

In short, there are two sides of the coin I want you to consider. First, please see if your school has a career office.

Go there at least once, check out their website and follow their social media accounts. I know you might not find exactly what you're looking for, but in my experience, those offices are full of people who truly want to help you—so give them a chance, even if it's out of your comfort zone.

Secondly, and you may not like hearing this: you are the only person responsible for your future. *Complaining about your lack of support won't do anything except keep you right where you are.* If you truly want more out of life—a better situation, a brighter future—it's up to you to make it happen. That doesn't mean other people won't help you. They will, but you have to ask for their help. You have to put yourself out there. I'll stop the lecturing, but only because I know you are capable. When there's something you really want, what will you do to make it happen?

I hear complaints about college career centers all the time, but The National Association of Colleges and Employers (NACE) found that, "college students who use career center services tend to receive more job offers than those who do not."[74]

To Have, or Have Not

I'd like to share a story about a student who made me think about things a bit differently. A couple of years ago, I got a resume from a recent college graduate that was four pages long. Seriously. It was essentially an unformatted list of everything the young man had done his entire life. Before you judge or try to rationalize, it did include some impressive accomplishments—leadership awards, clubs, community service, good grades, plus a few summer jobs and internships. He just had no idea how to put it all together in a professional format. Why? He went to a small regional school that didn't have a career center. It put him at such a disadvantage.

This got me thinking about all of the students who never step foot into their career center. What a gigantic missed opportunity that seems to be trending among current students. After all, it's part of what your tuition affords you.

Don't worry, I'm not here to scold you or argue about the quality of your guidance counselor, but I do want you to think about the resources you have available to you that you might be taking for granted.

Proactive or Bust

By way of example—and I can only speak directly about my experience with the universities I attended—I got tremendous value from the career centers at the University of Michigan and Emory University's Goizueta Business School. Generally, I think they are what you make of them. However, **if you're looking for specialized industry or function-specific support, you're going to have to carry a lot of the load yourself.** For example, most top business schools have on-campus recruiting machines for consulting and investment banking, but not for niche industries.

My high school class was only 125 people, so when I went to the University of Michigan I was nervous, daunted by the specter of a campus with over 30,000 students. Fortunately, I had enrolled in a program that was a bit smaller and had a much better ratio of support from the career center. As it turns out, "support" was quite an understatement as I was lucky to be assigned to a fantastic student advisor, Brad Brady. He was small in stature, quiet by nature, but big on listening.

During an advising session, I asked him if he had any ideas for internships that I could take on. After a moment of thought, he asked me if I'd be interested in partnering with a local business to plan a charity running race in Ann Arbor.

From there, Brad introduced me to one of my first mentors, Elmo Morales, who owned a legendary t-shirt shop on Main Street. For every ounce of Brad's reserved nature, Elmo was the opposite—a bundle of energy and ideas nearly exploding out of his every pore. By the spring of my sophomore year, we staged a two-mile event with dozens of participants, all organized by a handful of students, including my future wife. So, not only did Brad lead me to one of the early leadership experiences on my resume, but that event was also the beginning of the most important relationship of my life.

As if that wasn't enough value to speak of from the U of M career office, I was also blessed with a guardian angel who became another advisor, mentor, and still a friend to this day. Shelly Kovacs is one of a kind. The kindest kind of spitfire known to mankind, she has no doubt touched thousands of lives, including my own. As a sort of Jewish mom away from home, Shelly was always around for a shoulder to lean on or some tough love to get me unstuck, and out of my own way. To this day, Shelly has impacted our family as she became the college coach for our son as he prepared his college essays and applications. When I trust my kid's future to someone, you better believe they are special.

Lastly, there was Harry McLaughlin, a big guy who could pass as Santa Claus at a glance. Harry gave me a different kind of gift as a student. He taught one of my first courses at Michigan—Sports Management 101. I got a B in that class, and I was pissed. This was a topic I knew a lot about, I studied hard, and I didn't get the A that I thought I deserved. Why? Student participation was 25 percent of the grade, and I hadn't said a word all semester. I was angry at Harry, didn't think it was fair—how could "not talking" have a negative effect on my GPA?

It took some time, but I eventually realized that experience taught me some important lessons: read the syllabus, know the grading rubric, and participate in class! That jolt was exactly what I needed, and I will always appreciate Harry for getting my attention, and making me better. As a 19-year-old kid, I didn't realize that I would become a better student and leader by speaking up, and that the whole class benefits when more people participate. Now as an instructor myself, I truly get it and hope you find the courage to speak up and get a good discussion going. The college environment is a low-risk testing ground for this kind of interaction, and even asking a good question in class can get you out of your comfort zone in a way that paves your path to overcoming public speaking fears. Furthermore, everyone will benefit from your contribution, however small ... especially you.

In a way, history repeated itself when I got my MBA at Emory. One of the most valuable courses I ever took was called Goizueta Plus, a career navigation course required for all students, taught by Molly Epstein. Every Tuesday from 4:00 to 5:30 pm, this class helped us figure out our career path, prepare our resumes, and practice interviews. I look back at those Tuesday afternoons as some of the highest ROI hours of my life.

Not only did Molly prepare us for our first jobs out of business school, but I sat in her class and developed job search frameworks that I still use today with my coaching clients. In a serendipitous moment a couple of years ago, I was setting up my classroom for my first-ever paid teaching gig at Emory: *"Career Navigation in Sports, Media, and Technology."*

As I turned on my laptop and sorted out the projector, I heard a noise in the hallway, peeked my head out and saw Molly. What are the odds? I was about to teach a class, using resources I gleaned from her lessons 22 years prior, and got to thank her in person for the impact she had on my life. Molly officially retired from Emory last year, and I hope she's able to bask in the fact that she has had a similar ripple effect on thousands of students.

Creative Approaches

While I could point out many examples of problems in college career centers, there are plenty of schools that are approaching career readiness in novel ways. **Another option is to leverage external organizations and professionals to augment college career offices.** After all, there's only so much a few staff members can do to support thousands of students. Introships CEO, Joe Fiveash, says, "Large institutions are often too busy to engage; smaller private colleges like Davidson and Hampden-Sydney College have been more receptive" to exploring what their company has to offer.[75]

In particular, Fiveash says the University of Northern Colorado has been very open to collaboration, where Ben Moore is director of the Advising and Success Center. Moore says, "This is a way to get these students a lot of exposure to different careers, but maybe in a way where they don't have to be really out there aggressively job searching like they would have to for an internship. It just kind of made sense to give it a shot. We've given it a chance, and it seems to have gone well."[76]

Under Moore's leadership, UNCO also hosts an annual "Networking Night" to help students build professional skills in a low-risk environment. He's noticed a recent shift among students towards seeking more in-person, on-campus connections compared to previous years.

Jessica Santana is the inspiring CEO of America on Tech which is focused on preparing the next generation of technology leaders from underestimated communities. She sees a landscape among 18- to 25-year-olds that will require a collaborative approach across institutions, "I'd love to see more partnerships, more intentional relationship building, so we can really impact systems-level change, because if we each and every one of us stays in our own corners, it really doesn't bode well for the future."[77]

Santana continues with this lofty vision, "I believe we need a national talent strategy to solve issues around employment and career mobility for young people. Everyone plays a role here. It's not just one person's responsibility, it's everyone's responsibility."

Patrice Williams-Lindo is the CEO of Career Nomad, and she acknowledges that your potential lack of readiness for the job market isn't all your fault. "We've told an entire generation that if they played by the rules—study hard, pick the 'right' major, graduate on time—the market would reward them. That social contract is broken. And no amount of resume polishing will fix a structural mismatch between what institutions are producing and what industries are prioritizing."[78]

One model that addresses this gap in a very successful, practical way are five-year college plans that leverage co-op programs, including Northeastern and the University of Cincinnati which integrate practical work experience into their curriculums.

Northeastern's co-op program is often ranked Number One in the *U.S. by U.S. News & World Report.* As of 2024, 95 percent of Northeastern students participate in at least one co-op, which extends globally across all seven continents. The university has partnerships with Fortune 500 companies and startups, offering diverse and practical experiences. As a result, a high percentage of Northeastern graduates are employed or enrolled in further education within nine months of graduation, a testament to the program's effectiveness.[79]

The University of Cincinnati's co-op program partners with thousands of employers, including major companies like GE Aviation, Disney, Toyota, Kroger, and Procter & Gamble. According to the school, their students collectively earn $88 million annually.[80]

If you have the option, a college co-op can jump-start your career, help fund your education, and enable you to graduate with a degree in one hand and a career plan in the other—with the skills and competencies to launch a lifetime of careers.

Emory University features a unique, comprehensive approach to student success. The Pathways Center functions as a hub of five student-facing programs: career services, experiential learning, national scholarships and fellowships, pre-health advising and undergraduate research.

"From graduate and professional schools, to fellowships and jobs, whatever they choose to do, students can discover it through our space," says Branden Grimmett, an associate dean in Emory College and the leader of the Pathways Center.

Georgia State University in Atlanta is also ensuring that tomorrow's workforce is career-ready. Daniel Varitek (BBA '20) says he's proof that Georgia State's approach to career readiness works. After a 10-week internship at *The New York Times*, he spent four years in leadership in the company's marketing organization and today works on national marketing campaigns as a project manager with Verizon. "I gained the hard skills from my business degree—business analysis, designing marketing campaigns, even coding websites—but just as important were the soft skills: presenting, collaborating, and problem-solving," he said. "Honestly, I still think back to my GSU classes all the time. They gave me the confidence to show up, to lead, and to make an impact."[81]

"We're building much more of a career-readiness ecosystem," says Allison Calhoun-Brown, senior vice president for Student Success at Georgia State and the university's chief enrollment officer. "We're working to infuse and scale career experiences throughout the entire university."

Career Stress Support

Before leaving this topic, I want to come back to the stress and anxiety concerns you may experience. Some colleges are reimagining career services for students who prioritize mental health and well-being. "There are some students who get stressed out easily and prioritize taking care of themselves over being accountable," said Briana Randall, executive director of the Career & Internship Center at the University of Washington.[82]

Around the country, 486 institutions weave a set of "career competencies" into their curriculums, as developed by the National Association of Colleges and Employers (NACE). One of their courses, called "Career and Self-Development," delves into mental health and well-being. It explores, "how a student thinks through their whole self and what it means to have work-life balance," says NACE president and CEO Shawn VanDerziel.

Johns Hopkins University has changed how it supports students' career goals to help them build the meaningful lives they are looking for. "What Gen Z is asking for is, 'Provide me a work environment in which I can work and feel fulfilled,'" says Farouk Dey, the vice provost leading the shift toward a "Life Design" approach.

At the JHU Imagine Center, students can enjoy free hot chocolate in quiet spaces marked with words like hygge (Danish for coziness and living in the moment) and 'imi ola' (Hawaiian for seeking your best life). The support team focuses on eliciting student curiosity to help them explore their genuine interests.

A National Institutes of Health (NIH) study from 2022 underscores this consideration, entitled "Job-Seeking

Anxiety and Job Preparation Behavior of Undergraduate Students." Utilization of university job information sites and facilities is very important in lowering anxieties. Students could benefit from customized job preparation programs for each department.[83]

In addition to college career centers, **students are finding professors, club advisors, and tutors to be great resources for career support.**

A recent Indiana University graduate named Marnie found a lot of practical support from professors who had worked in the industry: "Most of my media school professors had a career in journalism before starting. They know what you can do, and that's why they would speak highly of you and help you." Marnie also found her club advisors helpful, "The director recently came out of a broadcasting job, and everything he taught us, it didn't come from a classroom. It came from him doing the job and just being there."[84]

Christina Alejandre of Lasell University is exactly one of those professors who came from industry and knows what the students need to be successful outside of the classroom. She underscores that, **"It's okay not to have everything figured out. Following a general direction is more important than having a detailed roadmap."**[85]

UVA faculty member, Kelsey Kubelick highlighted the availability of alumni networks, which provide valuable connections for students. She says, "It's really important to help students understand how to effectively utilize these resources."

Leslie and Libby Marx are a mother/daughter powerhouse who run Tutoring By A College Professor which has provided tutoring, career counseling, and life skills coaching to over 8,000 students nationwide and has over 600 tutors who can help students in all college-level subjects across all colleges and universities. They have noticed and filled a glaring gap in the ecosystem for one-to-one support that goes well beyond academic support.

Tutors have an inside track to a trusting relationship with students where they can maintain confidentiality, which can be important for young adults who are self-conscious about going to office hours. Leslie Marx, CEO of Tutoring By A College Professor, says, "The kids are reluctant to go to the job fairs. They don't want to be seen doing it because that announces to the world that they don't have a job yet."[86]

Leslie says their services, "really bridge the gap between high school and college for many of these students." This reflects a reality that TAs, professors, and even the career office don't have enough hours in the day to provide one-to-one support to all students.

Libby also advocates for patient perseverance along what can be a bumpy road, "If a door is closed to you, that just means that there's something better in store. **Keep believing in yourself, because anything that you invest in yourself is going to pay off.** It may not pay off in the way that you thought. I didn't get that job that I wanted, but I got a better job, for me."

Job Corps is another option for career path support. It's the nation's largest free, residential, career training and education program for low-income young adults ages 16 to 24. By offering hands-on training in fields like manufacturing, health care, technology, and construction, they prepare students for lifelong careers.[87]

These are just a handful of examples of creative approaches to career support that I'm sure will continue to flourish. If your career office doesn't provide similar opportunities, there are external organizations ready to help.

There may also be value in a gap year, study abroad, apprenticeship, part-time job, etc. You will have to invest the time to figure out what might work for you.

Coaching Question: What college career resources can you tap into that you haven't tried yet?

Section 4

Bad News/Good News

CHAPTER 9
Social Media

"Social media shows everyone's success, which can be stressful and hard to keep up with."

Max, 22-year-old college graduate in California

This is the first of three chapters involving themes that showed evidence of negative pressure *and* positive possibilities for young professional career journeys. I have a love/hate relationship with social media. One thing I love is the legitimate hilarity and creativity of people online. Historically, media was a unidirectional broadcast medium. The content from a few was distributed to the masses. Now, the content from the masses can be shared with the world. Not everyone is Jake Shane or Bobbi Althoff, but there are some gems out there. And those moments of pleasure, joy, happiness, and humor have value for my family's daily lives.

And then, there's the rabbit hole, the never-ending scroll, the bad actors, and the bed rotting. What the rabbit hole is doing to our brains is just beginning to be understood. There's an emotional reality behind LinkedIn-friendly milestones. It's not just about stress, it's about identity, betrayal, doubt, and resilience in a world that doesn't slow down for anyone under 30. It's a true existential crisis.

LinkedIn: Mandatory Misery?

From a career standpoint, most of this is exacerbated on LinkedIn. As with most platforms, people are portraying their best selves, manicured images to satisfy their supposed "followers" and their own egos. Self-preservation is a natural tendency, so I won't fault people for hustling. But the collective impact on the audience, especially young professionals, can be mentally draining and debilitating.

In survey results, 54 percent of respondents said LinkedIn increases their anxiety. 62 percent feel that "everyone's ahead but me" after scrolling through social media.[88] But you can't seem to break away—TikTok is now the "main source of career advice" for 47 percent of students.

Here are a few representative comments:

> *LinkedIn is my least favorite app right now. Everyone's posting all these things. You just have to remind yourself that it's not everyone at all.*
>
> 22-year-old recent female college graduate

> *"I think a lot of us are too comfortable on social media. So, my advice to people who are younger than me is, be careful what you're putting out. It does, in fact, stick around, and people do care.*
>
> 25-year-old female graduate school student, Atlanta, Georgia

> *Seeing everyone's success on LinkedIn makes me feel behind.*
>
> 22-year-old female college graduate, New York, New York

> *Social media is both inspiring and stressful—it's hard not to compare.*
>
> 20-year-old nonbinary college student, Seattle, Washington.

> *TikTok is a disease almost as much as it's fun to scroll and see random stuff.*
>
> Garrett, college graduate, New York City

I know you're locked into your feed—surfing, swiping, and drowning. As re-quoted by one interviewee, **"Comparison is the thief of joy."** You are not running anyone else's race. This is your life, not theirs. Are they making more money? Did they win an award you coveted? Is their house nicer than yours? So what! Try answering this question: Are they happy? Maybe, but possibly not. You've been raised on social media. You know how this game works. Nobody is posting everything. You have no idea what's going on behind their avatar or what they edit out. More than likely, they are only posting the good stuff, and most of it is a distortion of reality, at best.

In a Vice.com article entitled, "LinkedIn might be the worst social media app for Gen Z," one student says, "I don't even want to open LinkedIn," waffling between the stress of comparison and the value and need to be there to make professional progress.[89]

The author of *The Anxious Generation*, Jonathan Haidt, outlines four impact areas of smartphones on children: social deprivation, sleep deprivation, attention fragmentation, and addiction. He puts it bluntly, "TikTok is hurting kids." If you want to see this phenomenon in action, I'd recommend watching Lauren Greenfield's Emmy-nominated documentary TV series called "Social Studies." She followed teens around with video cameras and screen readers that captured their simultaneously online and offline lives in the context of school, home, and their social lives.

Watching these high schoolers experience waves of emotion as they confront stressful situations is disheartening, and it's clear that the virtual universe isn't helping. How you manage your time and attention is really important. Why? **Reducing social media leads to improved happiness.**[90] *The New York Post* spoke with several young professionals, and they all noted that limiting their time on Instagram, TikTok, and other social media platforms was crucial to their mental well-being.[91]

When discussing this challenge, one interviewee isolated the dichotomy—you are stressed out by comparing yourself to a fictional reality, *and* you are comforted when you realize your real life counterparts are in the same boat as you. That's what's real—you just have to remind yourself to look up from your phone and connect IRL with actual humans going through a similar life journey that comes with hurdles you will encounter and survive.

In particular, TikTok has risen as a career resource with over three-billion-total views across videos with the hashtags #CareerTok and #CareerAdvice.[92] If you are looking for the silver (or gold) lining of social media support, I've scoured the #CareerTok universe, and here are some accounts you might want to follow for specific, credible value:

@careercoachmandy (Mandy Tang)
Columbia MBA and career coach offers guidance on job changes, career pivots, and professional development.

@allifromcorporate0 (Allison Peck)
Specializes in helping early-career STEM professionals with job hunting, interviewing, and networking.

@rawantheplug (Rawan)
Noted for her supportive approach, especially toward underrepresented communities and those navigating

stressful career transitions. She creates content that acknowledges the emotional challenges of job searching and workplace stress.

@CareerConfidant (Gabrielle Woody)
Highlighted for her inclusive, supportive content. She addresses not just practical career advice, but also the emotional impact of workplace discrimination and stress, offering guidance on how to respond and cope.

@roxycouse
Focuses on first-generation college students, offering support and advice for those unsure about their career trajectory.

Content creation is also a double-edged sword. While one college student from Miami found his internship through Instagram DMs, a young female professional at Fox Sports named Nicolette believes social media has had a negative impact on younger generations. She highlights issues like unrealistic life comparisons, financial pressures, and the spread of harmful content. She proposed solutions such as regulating algorithms to reduce harmful content, promoting authenticity among creators, and developing apps to limit social media usage. Nicolette also emphasized the importance of us all doing our part to foster a more positive online environment devoid of trolling and bullying.[93]

Alternatives may be underway, according to entrepreneurs Nathaneo Johnson and Sean Hargrow who have secured VC funding to launch a product called Series that is intended to be "a healthy, meaningful, high-value platform to connect."⁹⁴ As Johnson says, "I built a platform for dreamers chasing big things. A platform proving that when you meet the right person at the right time—everything can change."

While not everyone can be the next Mr. Beast, there are still countless opportunities for exposure and professional success that haven't existed previously.

When I coach my clients about how to approach LinkedIn, it always starts with their goals. What are you trying to accomplish? How might LinkedIn fit into your branding or marketing strategy? I realize I just creeped out a bunch of people with that lingo. Not everyone thinks of themselves this way, or even needs to. None of this is mandatory, but I do want you to consider the possibility of tapping into an audience to help you define and achieve your career goals. You don't have to brag, you don't need to self-promote, and you don't have to be an arrogant asshole—actually, please don't. You can avoid all of those personas and just be yourself.

My coaching program includes a module called "Level Up on LinkedIn." There are four distinct stages that you have the option of graduating through.

The first is just **BUILDING A FOUNDATION**—a solid profile hygiene for anyone who might look up your profile—before an interview, before a meeting, or just in case a recruiter or hiring manager finds your profile while scouring for talent. It's the equivalent of brushing your teeth and hair before you leave your house in the morning. This includes the basics: a proper headshot, background, headline, about section and skills.

Level 2 is **CONNECT**—this is the beginning of engagement. Creating and maintaining connections. Connect with a fellow student right after you meet them in class. Connect with a guest speaker from a recent lecture. Connect with your professors, career counselors, parents, and friends. This is an organic and relevant way to build your audience without stepping too far out of your comfort zone. Note—do this with simple, personalized invitations to increase acceptance rates. A target of 500+ connections at graduation is a solid and realistic goal.

The third level is **CURATE**—as a result of the deluge of crappy content mentioned above, you can bring sanity to people's timelines by discovering and re-posting great content. You can elevate valuable events and resources. Even a short comment can bring quality content to people's feeds. You don't need to write much to be seen as someone adding value to the ecosystem.

Lastly, for the ambitious among you, is **CREATE**—write about something you know. Let people know about a topic where you have some confidence. Elevate the conversation, engage others, prompt thoughtful responses. Images, videos, and polls are all options for testing. See what feels right for you, then measure and iterate. Your voice will grow from there, and the results will speak for themselves.

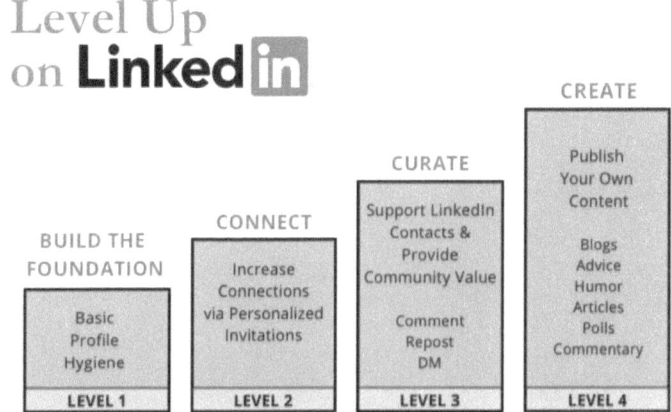

Coaching Question: How can you use social media for its benefits while limiting the harm?

CHAPTER 10
Artificial Intelligence

"Companies need to stop replacing entry level positions with AI"

23-year-old male college graduate, Oakley, California

Guess what the top two fastest-growing jobs are in the US, according to LinkedIn?[95]

- AI Engineer ranks number one globally, jumping from lower rankings last year
- AI Consultant follows closely at number two, reflecting the rapid integration of AI across industries

The rest of the list is also telling, with "human-centric" roles gaining steam:

- At number three, Physical Therapist underscores the enduring need for hands-on care
- Workforce Development Manager and Travel Advisor round out numbers four and five, pointing to the demand for skills AI can't replace

LinkedIn is also seeing a surge in frontline and service-oriented roles like Research Librarian, Security Guard, and Flight Attendant, driven by post-pandemic trends in travel, aviation, and entertainment.[96]

Can't Stop, Won't Stop

AI is coming fast ... faster than any career-impacting technology I've ever seen. I was around as the nascent internet disrupted many industries. I also saw the rise of mobile technology and apps, and the onset of social media proliferation, which enabled a user-generated content revolution, in some cases quite literally. AI is different; it's already changing the foundational methods of learning and doing business. Of marketing, and analysis. Of distribution and creativity. I could go on and on. Let's examine this in two parts—the related increase in career uncertainty and the bright spots where you can find hope.

According to a study conducted by Indeed, "51% of Gen Z Views Their College Degree as a Waste of Money."[97] This point of view suggests a need for "rethinking education for an AI-driven world."

Their parents are concerned, too—even parents like AI Transformation Strategist Garth Case, who says, "My son graduates college in two years. I'm terrified for him. Not because he lacks talent or drive. But because we're systematically removing the bottom rungs from the career ladder we've all climbed." He goes on to say, "We're eliminating the very roles that teach critical thinking, relationship building, and institutional knowledge. We're creating a generation of AI-powered companies run by executives who never learned these fundamentals. The question isn't whether AI will transform work— it's whether we'll be intentional about preserving pathways for human development in the process."[98]

What do you think will be the effect of AI on your generation? How will it evolve?

Being stressed out about the job market right now is normal, and AI is only partially to blame. The 2025 Future of Jobs report by the World Economic Forum found that 48 percent of U.S. employers worldwide intend to reduce their workforce because of AI within the next five years. However, the report also forecasts a net gain of new jobs, suggesting that **AI's impact is more about transforming the landscape than outright job elimination.**[99]

So what paths offer some optimism? The first option may be more obvious than you realize—working with AI. People are needed to inform and harness artificial intelligence for business purposes. Developing AI literacy is critical to understanding what's possible and becoming someone in your organization who can do what has always been valued—create growth or find efficiencies.

Embracing and Outpacing the Robot Revolution

What skills or roles are "AI-proof"? As implied by the data points above, I think it's the human ones. Communication, collaboration, influence, empathy ... to name a few. I also believe the human capacity for creativity is irreplaceable. That might sound a tad naive or wishful thinking, but I haven't seen anything solely AI-generated that made me laugh or cry uncontrollably. Music, art, and great writing still have a way of penetrating surface-level emotions and creating intense inspiration.

Author and tech leader, Dr. Stacey Rivers addresses the value of emotional intelligence, or EQ, in her book, *Career Smarts for College Students:*

> *The significance of emotional intelligence and other interpersonal skills have become crucial to a company's competitive advantage. Beyond technical expertise, suc-*

cess in one's career hinges on understanding complex social landscapes and forming meaningful connections with colleagues, clients, and stakeholders. Emotional intelligence, which includes self-awareness, self-regulation, empathy, and interpersonal skills, is the cornerstone of effective communication and collaboration.[100]*

Rivers continues:

Professionals with high emotional intelligence can navigate conflicts with finesse, foster a positive work environment, and adapt to diverse team dynamics. These skills are instrumental in building strong leadership, fostering teamwork, and establishing a culture of trust within organizations. In an era where collaboration and innovation are paramount, individuals who prioritize emotional intelligence and interpersonal skills will not only thrive personally, but will contribute significantly to their workplace's overall success and harmony.

As AI and automation began to become apparent solutions for efficiency, I was confronted with my own conflict as a department head in the early 2020s. There was absolutely going to be value in integrating new tools into our workflows, but my first fear was on behalf of my staff: *Would I automate their jobs away?* I'm sure they were thinking it, too, just like you are now. The truth was that a lot of their work was manual, tedious, and time consuming. They didn't enjoy those parts of their jobs anyway, so it was really a matter of finding opportunities to leverage their strategic mindset and creativity as a result of the productivity gains.

The World Economic Forum also indicated there is some upside opportunity for you and your co-workers overcoming the AI surge, identifying The Core Skills for 2030[101]:

- Analytical thinking
- Resilience, flexibility & agility
- Leadership & social influence
- Motivation & self-awareness
- Creative thinking
- Systems thinking
- Curiosity & lifelong learning

One challenge is that you may have been dissuaded from using AI in academic settings as administrators weren't sure how to deal with the proliferation, especially as it relates to plagiarism and student shortcuts for homework assignments. However, academia is starting to come around to the fact that you need to know how to harness AI to be relevant in the future marketplace. And of course, you were always playing with it anyways, right?

Workforce expert and author, Ken Taylor has also identified another area of opportunity. He says, "There is also significant scope for regulated jobs. For example, my son is pursuing civil engineering - there's no way that building codes will allow AI signoff for plans anytime soon, that will require a fully-qualified engineer for a long time to come."[102]

From a career development standpoint, you likely use AI tools like ChatGPT for career advice, with several of you noting: "I use Reddit and GPT more than real people."

One 20-year-old student in San Francisco says, "I wish there were more AI tools that could help match my interests to careers. It's overwhelming to search on my own." Those are coming out fast and furious now, in a way that this book won't be able to keep up with, but I've listed some current resources below that provide a good starting point if you aren't already tinkering with new tools.

AI Tools for Career Transition:

- **Stay vs Quit**
  tealhq.com/tools/stay-vs-quit-job-quiz
- **Google Career Dreamer**
  grow.google/career-dreamer/home/
- **Ikigai GPT**
  chatgpt.com/g/g-kaNVjduOL-ikigai-gpt
- **ONet Interest Profiler**
  onetcenter.org/
- **LinkedIn Headline Generator**
  taplio.com/headline-generator
- **Enhancv Resume Creator**
  enhancv.com
- **Sorce - Tinder for Jobs**
  sorce.jobs
- **JennieJohnson Application Tracker**
  jenniejohnson.com
- **FinalRound AI - Interview simulator**
  finalroundai.com

New challenges will also emerge, indicated by these insightful quotes:

> *AI resume builders have made applying easier, but I worry everyone's using the same templates.*
> 22-year-old male college grad in Chicago

> *ChatGPT helped me prep for interviews, but sometimes I'm not sure if the advice is realistic.*
> 21-year-old nonbinary college student from Miami

In a commencement speech to the Temple University College of Liberal Arts class of 2025, renowned Tech Journalist Steven Levy reassured graduates that despite the rise of AI, their education remains valuable and relevant. Although he acknowledged the rapid advancements in AI, he explained that no matter how advanced it gets, it cannot replicate uniquely human connections, empathy, or consciousness.[103]

Here's a question I asked myself recently: **What fears or hopes do I carry for the next generation growing up with AI as a normal part of their world?**

My immediate answer to this introspection was that you will resist human connection at the expense of AI convenience. In a way this is like using a calculator or Excel instead of your brain to do simple math. Adopting new technology is great, but not at the expense of forgetting how to think critically (or never learning how in the first place).

I think handshakes matter. So does looking people in the eye. Collaborating. Laughing together. Crying together. Listening, deeply. After all, if you're not spending time with other people, then other people aren't spending time with you. How about we value IRL over the URL? Don't you want hugs, smiles, and winks? A shoulder to lean on, empathy and understanding, relatability and storytelling, reflection and adaptation, suggestion vs deference?

And what will happen to creativity itself, as you use available crutches for your first drafts, or 10th revision? In my mind, writing is equivalent to thinking. How will you create words out of your thoughts that can influence or inspire others if you depend on AI, which doesn't (yet) read your thoughts? Do you think AI-generated music will exceed the human spark that your favorite entertainers delight you with?

Are you destined for a life of avoidance?
Avoiding the cashier at Starbucks
Avoiding eye contact with a waiter
Avoiding social activities
Avoiding office hours with your professor
Avoiding the career center
Avoiding your parents

Are you really going to let a computer, designed by humans, decide how you will live your life?

What life will you live if every decision you make originates from a machine?

Coaching Question: What is the price of disconnecting from humanity?

CHAPTER 11
Family

"My family expects me to succeed, but their definition of success isn't mine."

22-year-old female college graduate,
San Antonio, TX

"My parents just don't get it!" A recent college grad said this to me in our first session last week. It's become cliché—basically a right of passage. Who hasn't thought that parents don't understand our lives, what we're going through, or how to help? "It would be better if they just shut up because everything they say is just so irritating."

Okay, maybe it's not that harsh ... or sometimes maybe it's worse. Either way, even if you have a family that you know loves you and cares about you, it's still hard to accept their advice.

As our son prepared to leave for college a few years ago, it felt like a gigantic milestone. He's our oldest child and had grown up before our eyes—learning to crawl, walk, talk, and run. Not only did he find his footing, he also found his voice. In parallel, while he was finding his own way, we were learning to let go. I think the reason this transition is hard for parents is because it feels good to be needed, and when your kids don't seem to need you as much, you lose some of your identity. As I said in the introduction, I've directed this book at your generation. I can't deny that part of my rationale for that direction was to better understand my own kids—how they're feeling about the universe, themselves, and their careers.

One thing I'll ask you to keep in mind as your parents' lives transform, is to realize that you will always be their children. You are an adult, but to them, you are still their child. As stated in the book *Quarterlife Crisis* by Abby Wilner and Alexandra Robbins, **"In the eyes of your parents you can never stop being a kid."**[104]

And if your parents show their love by wanting to be involved in your life, I hope you'll recognize their love and let them help you—at least every once in a while. That doesn't mean you have to follow their dreams—you have your own. But, if you can find a way to communicate with them about your aspirations, it can be a powerful way to unlock a future of mutual respect.

With that background, I want to share something personal with you. This is a letter my wife and I sent to our son as he headed to college in Athens, Georgia in August, 2022. It was our attempt to acknowledge his growth and support him in a new way going forward.

> To Brandon, as you leave for college:
>
> In some ways, the last two years have prepped us for what's to come. Of course, you needed us when you were little, and we were there for you. As you got older, you needed us less, and you needed your space more. When you turned 13, you retreated into yourself in a way that was surprising. Not because you loved us any less. That's never been in question. But the role of a parent changes over time. Your self-reliance was actually the greatest compliment. We provided a stable foundation, and that's the best springboard anyone can hope for. The rest is about letting go. Sleepovers, camp, spring break, road trips. This isn't your first time away. We've had more than enough practice walking past your empty room. You have achieved big wins on your own, and you will continue to do so.
>
> Your safety net will never disappear—it will just be 64 miles away, someday maybe even further. But you can always find us in an instant, and we will be there. We will never stop loving you, missing you, nudging you. We will say "be careful" a million more times because let-

ting go is scary. But the choices are yours, and we trust you. You are amazing, kind, and smart, and we are so proud of you.

We know the next chapter is starting. There is no stopping it. We will support the choices you make and the path you decide to follow. This life is yours to explore. We know it will take you to many unexpected places. All we hope is that you continue to flourish, learn, laugh, and call home to share your experiences with us. Cutting the cord is hard, but we promise to let you live your life. We will always be your biggest cheerleaders.

We love you. Have the best time at UGA.

Mom and Dad

I don't know what his reaction was to this heartfelt note, but it was probably as much a benefit to our own conscience as anything.

Family plays a complex and dual role in the career stress experience of young adults aged 18 to 25. A majority, 52 percent, of students say their parents are their main source of both support and stress. Understanding this nuanced duality is critical for designing effective career counseling, managing anxiety, and providing support networks tailored to young adults' needs.

Here is a summary of my survey findings about family relationships as they relate to career pursuits:

FAMILY RELATIONSHIP TO CAREER STRESS

STRESS SOURCE
Family expectations for a career path not aligned with your goals or interests

STRESS RELIEF
Family time is a top coping strategy for emotional support

CAREER PRESSURE
Family pressure linked to expectations of success on a particular timeline

CAREER SUPPORT
Family support is beneficial for career advice and networking

High stress levels are strongly associated with respondents who list "Family" or "Living up to parent expectations" as a main cause of stress. This effect is especially pronounced among women, nonbinary, Hispanic/Latino, and Black respondents, with 68 percent saying family pressure was a "major stressor." Also notable is that family-related stress tends to increase with career progression and correlates with financial stress.

You Know What You Know

While I ended up having a very fulfilling career in the sports media industry, I almost became a doctor. Why? Because my father was a doctor. It's what I knew. He loved his job, he helped people, he was respected, he made money. That sounded pretty good to me. Although he was a pediatrician, my first instinct was to go into sports medicine. I have been a sports fan my whole life and was an athlete growing up—in swimming, football, and track. Long story short, swimming stretched out my joints and took advantage of my flexibility ... then I chose to cross-train with football, including time as a defensive back/safety, which involved significant physical contact. Eventually enough tackles led to several shoulder dislocations. I was devastated to see the end of my career aspirations, but it also opened my eyes to the fascinating world of orthopedics, which was my initial hypothesis for a career direction.

Here's an excerpt I found in my high school newspaper in January of my senior year—proof that I was still in the midst of this thought process.

> *If I end up in the University of Michigan, I'll be in a program called 'Kinesiology.' It deals with engineering and*

structural maintenance of most any type of machine, usually the human body. Actually, it's more about the way the muscles work together, and less about anything mechanical and man-made. It's hard to explain. Stop me in the halls sometime and I'll tell you all about it.

Basically, from this, I can take one of three routes—I can go into sports medicine, coaching, or athletic directing. Obviously, sports medicine would be the best in terms of income, but there's more to life than money, as I noticed in my coaching days this summer. If I coached for the rest of my life, it would be like merging my vocation and my avocation.

Not one word about sports management, or sports media, but it was a theory and got me headed in the right direction. And the part about coaching, well, you can see how that eventually worked out. Anyhow, while I was a pretty good student, I didn't love school and couldn't imagine a dozen more years of education after high school. Now, more than 30 years later, I can see how a painful injury led to an incredibly fulfilling career.

Family influence isn't just about parents either. My grandfather and uncle had both worked in the media industry, which could have been part of my subconscious decision-making, as well. Your professional worldview is impacted by your grandparents, aunts, uncles, siblings, and cousins, too. What you know is what you know. It's not a surprise that so many people choose paths similar to that of a close family member. It's what's in front of you—paths blazed by your role models, success stories on the horizon—that are so much easier to envision than nebulous options that haven't even crystallized yet in your own mind."

It might also explain why you've chosen to go down a different path, as exemplified by Caydence Bach, now a second-year student in Ann Arbor, "I want to go into an industry that my family is not in at all. My mom's an orthodontist, and my dad's a lawyer, both of which are very, very great professions. They did a lot of school and worked hard to get where they are. But that wasn't my path. So when I told them I wanted to go into the sports business, it was kind of like a question mark, like, *what does that mean?*"

A 21-year-old business major from Pomona, California is under a specific type of pressure. She says, "My parents want me to take over the family business, but I want something different." Or how about the expectations placed on the 20-year-old first-generation healthcare major from Detroit who says, "I'm the first in my family to go to college, so there's a lot of pressure."

You also might be putting extra pressure on yourself. 58 percent of Gen Zs expect to be more financially successful than their parents, according to a new Harris Poll on behalf of TD Ameritrade.[105]

One student says, "I don't want to let my family down. I don't want to waste this education because the tuition's so expensive."

Of course, there's also an upside to having the support of your family. Here's a good example from Ashton, a 26-year-old in Atlanta:

> *(I can be) completely vulnerable with my mother or my sisters, letting them know, like, hey guys, I'm really stressed out. I don't really feel like talking today. Or, hey guys, can I talk to you about something that happened at work, and have you ever dealt with the same situation? If so, how did you approach that, or if not, how would you approach it. How would you deal with that? Just so I know how to navigate those stressful situations.*[106]

You'll remember Dr. Stacey Rivers and her book, *Career Smarts for College Students*. In it, she reminds us that family can be the networking hook-up you need to move forward. "When we had our virtual family reunion, I learned I have relatives who are doctors, school principals, business owners, and high-ranking military officers. I didn't know some of them until 2020. Although a few are family by marriage, nevertheless, they are family. Now, I can access people with expert knowledge in areas I never considered."

And, when all else fails, you can call your mom. There's even research from the University of Wisconsin-Madison that supports the value of hearing your mother's voice. "Hearing your mother's voice has the potential to reduce stress. When young girls speak to their moms in person or by phone, oxytocin increases and cortisol decreases."

And for what it's worth, texting did not provide the same benefits.[107]

A Note For Your Parents or Guardians ...

If you're a student or young professional reading this, you might not know how to approach your parents or guardians for a serious discussion about your career stress. You can literally send a picture of this section to them if they don't already have a copy of the book themselves. In any case, I believe most parents are talking to you about your career because they care. They love you and are showing interest which is better than apathy any day.

Or, you might share some of the insights below on a selective basis. Whatever works for you is worth a shot as opening the door to honest communication could be exactly what you need to move your relationship from stress-inducing to stress relief.

Below are some resources, insights and suggestions that you can review and utilize as you see fit. Every parent/child relationship is unique, so I'm hoping you at least find one nugget that can help you both succeed.

Dr. Satya Doyle Byock is an Oregon-based psychotherapist who focuses on counseling young adults. In her book, *Quarterlife*, she says, "Parents must evolve. Parents of Quarterlifers also need to evolve their understanding and approach. Healthy Quarterlife development requires individuals to separate from parental dependence and influence, which can be challenging if parents struggle to let go or base their identity solely on parenthood. Parents can support this by focusing on their own psychological growth and modeling self-responsible living, allowing their children to find their unique path."[108]

Rebecca Winthrop, Director of the Center for Universal Education at the Brookings Institution, and Jenny Anderson, award-winning journalist, are co-authors of the influential education and parenting book *The Disengaged Teen*.[109] They provide three takeaways for parents to consider:

> 1. **Nudge don't nag** – too much criticism has the opposite effect, discouraging and unmotivating (this can be done by adjusting communication ever so slightly, rephrasing the question)

> 2. **Focus more on the learning rather than the performance** – too much emphasis on success discourages learning

> 3. **Shift focus from "find your passion" to "explore interests"** – it all starts with an interest or hobby

Dr Lisa Demour is a New York Times bestselling author of *The Emotional Lives of Teenagers*. On the Kate Bowler podcast, she talks about one of her chapters that answers the age old question - *Why does my kid hate how I chew?* "Everything you do is just so annoying to them. You're the worst. This is really separation and individuation doing its job. They are trying to establish their own brand."[110]

Even so, Demour says you can find a way to introduce civility to the dialogue. "You can say to them you have three options for how you can interact with me: you can be pleasant, that's my favorite. You can be polite. Or you can tell me you need space. Everything else is off the table."

This is kind of funny, but it's also not. I've been there. Maybe it's not your unconscionable habits at the dinner table, but teenagers are designed to question their parents and disregard everything we have to say. This isn't their fault. They didn't do anything wrong. Even in my 50s, I find myself feeling this way towards "silly" things my mom says. I don't even know why, it's just in our programming to resist our parents' wisdom, to set out on our own, to prove we can support ourselves. Parents shouldn't blame their kids for this if they act the same way. Their job is to love you unconditionally and if you become a parent yourself, you might eventually understand where they were coming from. You might even apologize.

Coaching Question: What content from this book could help you explain your career stress to your family members?

Section 5

Adulting

CHAPTER 12
Reality Check

I thought getting a degree would guarantee a job, but the real world is so much tougher.

24-year-old engineering graduate, Boston, Massachusetts

If you've just left high school, you might be anxious, but also hopeful and idealistic as you set out on new pastures, new adventures, in new surroundings. I love this idealism — it's a great recipe for dreaming, and I'm all for it. The sky is the limit, an ever-expanding universe, anything is possible! That does lead to a belief of what might be, the many paths of pursuit, the belief that passion can intersect with profession. And, while this might be a bit overly optimistic, I do encourage it, because I believe in infinite possibilities based on my own experience of a successful career in a very competitive field.

Conversely, as I talked to young professionals closer to their mid-twenties, just a few years later, they've now hit some walls that are seemingly insurmountable. Rainbows and unicorns haven't surfaced. Or, you got what you wanted and it wasn't what you expected. You encountered shitty bosses, disrespect, no glamour, muted passion, hard work, and long hours. You felt underutilized and overworked. Sitting at a desk is harder than you expected, and nobody is listening to your ideas. Do you feel like you're stuck in an episode of *Severance*?

One theme I've taken away from my research is the significant difference in perspectives between the younger and older ends of the age group I'm studying. Of course, this is pretty obvious, but the root of the insight is based on one concept—**reality check**. This is the foundational platform on which "Adulting" is placed. The journey from adolescence to adulthood comes with a rapid series of decisions and obligations previously taken for granted. It's not your fault, it's just the truth.

Here's one survey response that you might relate to: "The majority of my career-related stress comes from feeling a lack of security in my position. The feeling of disposability has me feeling on edge and as if I'll be cast aside unless

I'm consistently giving 110 percent," says a 25-year-old HR professional in Maryland.

One trend I've seen from high performers is that you've been superstars in high school and college, but didn't realize you were operating in a protective bubble. You became team captain, club president, a top-of-your-class performer. That's great, but entry level jobs elicit a level of humility you might not have experienced in a long time. You will encounter office bullies, limited praise, and deaf ears.

An article in the *Greenville Journal* from 2016 defines a quarterlife crisis as someone "in their 20s or 30s experiences overwhelming stress and anxiety regarding the transition into adulthood. It is commonly accompanied by fear of making the wrong choices and a feeling that everyone else has it all figured out."[111]

This rings true based on the research I've conducted, as well.

Cydney says, "I'm wondering if my vision for my career is even valid or makes any sense, or if it's the right path. It's just a lot of internal doubt and anxiety."

Alexa even worries about reaching her goals, "What if I get there in that career and I actually don't like it? That's also another fear that weighs on me."

Even once you have a job, you might be thinking about the next move, like Brooke: "Now I'm at the point where I feel like I am not using myself to my fullest potential."

Mallom, a film major from California, now 26, says, "A lot of your twenties is (finding out that) every job is so different than what it looks like from the outside, and it requires so many things that you can only be aware of in participating in that job."[112]

The good news is that **life isn't over at 25**. You still have plenty of time to pivot, and your skills and experience are transferable. It may not be apparent to you now, but if you dig into what you've learned and how you've grown, you are not the same kid anymore. And while you may not want to hear it, the disappointment you're going through is life's greatest teacher, in the form of life's most important skill: resilience.

Get knocked down nine times, get up ten. At age 25, you can change jobs, change industries, change locations. Like many people, you might not love change, but this is change on your terms. What is your strategy? What else might you enjoy? Where has demand shifted since college, and how can you reposition yourself for growth? You can also re-train, build new strengths, and go after something new.

Author Cate LeSourd experienced this transformation herself recently as she pivoted into a new career path. "I'm very grateful to say after graduating from a social work program that *I didn't realize how much I could actually feel more like myself in a career.* It doesn't quite feel like work in the same ways, and so it has provided a contrast to how lost and unfit I felt before."

The Value of Advanced Degrees

When I was 25, I thought my career hit a dead end while working for the Fulton County government television station. It was sad, painful, troubling, and discouraging. I wondered every day if I had gone down the wrong path. I wasn't growing, learning, or leading. Should I have taken that other job offer when I was 22? Did I make a huge mistake? What do I do now? Will I be able to support a family? I didn't hate my job, but the "good enough for government" vibe wasn't working for me.

This is a tough consideration for many, since you and your family may not have the financial resources to fund another round of education. Loans are possible, as are more affordable alternatives such as trade school or even the military. You might have access to a 529 plan, or unused benefits from the GI Bill. On the grad school option specifically, it depends what programs you are considering, but below is how I recommend approaching grad school, online programs, or any advanced certificates.

I believe there are four major benefits to weigh against the cost:

> **1. Classroom Learning** - depending on the courses and professors, what new skills or knowledge will you gain that can help you get a desired job or perform better in a role that you desire?

2. Practical/experiential learning - this is your chance to tackle school projects with real companies that can become potential employers, or at least solid interview answers.

3. Credibility - how much credibility will a certificate from this university have in the marketplace?

4. Network – What new people will you meet during or after the program by being affiliated with the university?

Lastly, what is the opportunity cost of the investment of time and money? In other words, what else could you do with that time and money that might be even more advantageous? Virtual programs might help manage costs while you level up your marketability.

I also have to raise a theory I've deduced from undergrads who are not sure what to do after commencement—grad school as a stall tactic. Is this on your mind? With a justifiable fear of rejection in the job market and lack of a confident trajectory, I don't blame you for this side quest. However, if you run your decision-making filter against the criteria above, you can also extract maximum value out of your extra education which can further inform your next move. If you are stalling, how can you best use your time to gain clarity and pursue a path that feels right to you?

For my wife and myself, the decision to get an MBA was financially driven and something we wanted to do before we started raising a family. I didn't want to hit a ceiling at some point in my career that was limited by not having an advanced degree. I also remember thinking about this when filling out surveys, that I wanted to be able to check the "Masters Degree" box. I don't know why, but I was always driven to achieve more.

One key milestone when you turn 26 years old is the bureaucratic reality of losing health insurance. Most companies allow you to stay on your parents' insurance plan through the age of 25. This is a major "adulting" wake up call. I've had three young clients go through this rite of passage recently ... and it's a doozy.

The exciting thing from my perspective is that when you are confronted with this conundrum, when your back is against the wall, you rise to meet the challenge. You do the research on your healthcare options, you learn about the marketplace or affordable alternatives. You get a part-time job to help cover some bills, while you still pursue your passion or further your education. There are options for overcoming adversity and sometimes it's the brick wall you face in front of you that inspires creative solutions. As has been said, necessity is the mother of invention.

Sydnee Walker is a great example of this scrappiness. She's currently working part-time at Bleacher Report as a social media programmer, paying for healthcare out-of-pocket after recently turning 27. Despite applying to numerous jobs and freelance contracts, she hasn't received a full-time offer. Sydnee is one of the best networkers I know and her resume and credentials are stellar. She's even the

CEO of The Collaborative, a non-profit organization that connects young professionals with seasoned veterans in the Sports and Entertainment industry.

She says several members of The Collaborative have found success through in-person events with corporate hosts, "It's a really great opportunity for them to be in front of these hiring managers, in front of people at the company, to learn more and potentially land a role. We hosted an event with the Atlanta Braves two years ago, and we ended up having two people at those events get roles with the team."[113]

I would guess that some of you have seen your parents go through a layoff. They've been fired, let go, or taken a package. The language changes, but the result is the same—you've witnessed a family member take a punch. How they responded is instrumental to your worldview. If they bounced back or made a pivot to a better place, that's part of your knowledge. If they took more time to get back on their feet, that's impactful too. You only know what you know, and your relatives' work experiences are fundamentally instrumental to your consciousness.

Timing is Relative

Many of you may have also fallen behind a certain schedule that you had envisioned for your life. You reached your mid-twenties, and you didn't have the things you wanted. You didn't achieve the level you'd expected. You weren't the person you hoped to become.

Some of this is society's fault; pop culture, TV shows, and other media fuel unrealistic expectations. Did you binge *Friends* during the pandemic? How the heck do you think they afforded their gigantic Manhattan apartment in their twenties? Take a closer look at their professions and estimate their income—there's no way they could pay the rent and wear all those nice clothes. The setup for *New Girl* is also a farce. I think Sydney's character in *The Bear* is a more realistic view of post-college professional life with grand aspirations.

I also believe the pandemic led to a normalized pursuit of passion and purpose, but you were not educated about the trade offs. You can go after your dreams, but it's going to be a grind. Where else do you think your expectations come from?

Many of you might be comparing your career progress to your parents' progress at the same age, which can lead to "false benchmarks." I think the situation is even more skewed than you might realize. As you've grown, you might only be familiar with your parents at their peak career stage—as successful executives with impressive titles who've been afforded a certain lifestyle. But they've struggled, too.

They might not talk about it. Maybe their tough years were before you were born, or when you weren't old enough to see it, or just didn't notice. I hope they talk to you about those times, reminding you that it's not an easy path. The struggle is real, and it helps to hear they can empathize with your endeavors. If you're not hearing this context, that's where mentors and advisors can be a huge advantage.

Coaching Question: How do you want to react when life throws you a curveball?

CHAPTER 13
Financial Stress

If I don't get a job soon, I won't be able to pay rent.
24-year-old engineering graduate,
Austin, Texas

One of the eye-opening benefits of mentoring dozens of students in my life is that I've seen life through their eyes—your eyes. Often, a much different life than I experienced. A life where you have to work at a restaurant while you go to school and scramble for an internship that fits your work and family schedule. Where you have to help raise your younger siblings because your single mother is working a night shift. Where you don't have the "right" clothes to wear to an interview and fear that you are being judged by your appearance before you even have a chance to prove how qualified you are. I didn't experience these challenges, but I know them, and I do my best to feel them. It's one of the reasons I'm writing this book, to do what I can to level the playing field, to impart any wisdom I've gathered, and to help everyone, even if you can't afford your own private career coach.

The data speaks for itself in a way many of you probably understand far better than I ever could:

- 68 percent of survey respondents listed financial pressure as their number one concern.
- 70 percent of college seniors with student debt say looming repayments will impact their career plans.[114]
- 48 percent of adults with a bachelor's degree said they took out student loans for their education.[115]
- 48 percent of Gen Zs say they do not feel financially secure.[116]

One early glimpse I had into the lives of students who had financial stress was when I was a board member for an organization called the Urban Youth Racing School. UYRS is a Philadelphia-based program that introduces inner-city youth to the world of motorsports and STEM (science, technology, engineering, and mathematics) fields. Founders Anthony and Michelle Martin leverage kids' excitement about racing into an after-school program that fosters educational growth through hands-on activities, and the history of motorsports, with the goal of inspiring kids to pursue careers in related fields.

Opportunity Knocks

Another organization I partnered with for several years is the Cristo Rey Jesuit School. Every summer between 2018 and 2022, our department hosted a few high school students as part of a work study program. Each student would come to the office one full day per week and perform a variety of tasks. It wasn't the same as having a college intern—some of these kids were freshmen, only 14 years old.

I distinctly remember the first time meeting one of them, Mario, and he had raced from the MARTA train to our offices in the rain. His uniform dress pants were soaked, and the first endearing story he told me was about his grandma who lived with him and his family. Mario was passionate about video games, and we had an e-sports division at the time so we were able to funnel him a project to analyze that marketplace and share his opinions of the gaming industry, top games, and promising publishers. It's one of the best projects I've ever had from any intern, much less such a young teen. His promise has materialized as he's about to graduate from Georgetown University this Spring.

One more student that comes to mind is Jose, a high school junior, the oldest of three brothers. He was actually the first intern I was able to manage from Cristo Rey.

When I signed up as a mentor for the program, one of my colleagues said, "He will have as much of an impact on you as you have on him." And he was right. That summer was a whirlwind—we were going through tremendous change as a company and doing our best to continue the growth we had experienced for decades.

An internal culture-building initiative that I'll always remember was called "Make You Matter Week." Employees around the company were able to participate in workshops that enabled professional development and new ways of thinking. As the industry was encountering headwinds, it was imperative that we all did our part to level up and bring more creativity to our efforts. When Jose arrived on one of those days, we attended a seminar called "The Six-Word Memoir."

The speaker was Larry Smith, the author of a book by the same name. Oddly enough, he was Piper's real-life husband in the breakout Netflix series Orange is the New Black. Anyhow, the purpose of the exercise was to think about the legacy we wanted to leave. What six words would you want on your tombstone? We separated into breakout groups, brainstorming and pondering such a heavy question.

After several drafts, Jose and I shared our memoir statements with each other. I thought mine was pretty good, and this pretty well sums up my approach to helping others—"I see the best in you." It felt good to say it, and it feels even better to live it. Then, Jose shyly showed me what he had written down: "Mexican parents are the best kind." Wow. So powerful. So succinct. So mature. At first I smiled, and then the corners of my eyes got a little wet.

At the end of that summer, we had a catered dinner celebration with the students and their families. I was able to meet his brothers and his mom that night. And when I had a chance to make a speech, I talked about the great experience I had with Jose. How hard he worked. How much he cared. How much I learned. Then, I slowly unrolled the poster Jose had created in the memoir seminar and showed it to his mom. Teary eyes and hugs all around. I definitely learned as much from him as he did from me. These students may not have the same financial support that I had when I was growing up, but they were able to be part of a program that allowed them to shine, gain confidence, and see a potential future they didn't even know was possible a few months before.

Based on my survey results, minority groups tend to report higher stress from financial concerns and family expectations. A 20-year-old female college student in San Antonio says, "Financial aid isn't enough, and my family can't help." Yet today, she's halfway to her college degree.

That pressure continues post-graduation with the concerns around paying off debt, including a 23-year-old female in Detroit who graduated with a bachelor's degree in healthcare. "I worry about student loans more than anything else," she said. This challenge often clashes with career goals.

If you cannot afford college, it's not the only option, says Deja White, CEO of Breakroom Buddha. "While college can be valuable, it's not always necessary, especially for fields that don't require specific degrees. Technical schools, bootcamps, and certifications can also provide valuable training."[117]

Regardless, wanting to be better off financially is pretty universal. There's an inclination to always want more, regardless of your situation. As stated by one respondent, "Desire for wealth forces you into jobs you don't want." Rent and job insecurity, especially in high-cost areas like Los Angeles, New York, and San Francisco, increase financial stress. Some of you know this problem goes deeper than most people realize. Even in small and mid-sized cities, rent has far outpaced income levels and buying a property is completely out of reach for most.

An Unbalanced Budget

As reported by the Department of Treasury in 2024, "For the past two decades, rents and house prices have been rising faster than incomes across most regions of the United States."[118]

Here's a chart from that same report which compares the housing and rental prices to median household income:

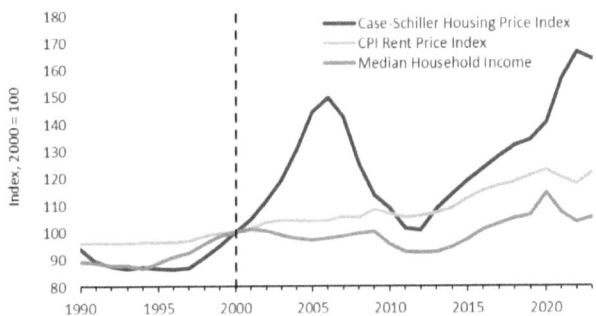

Note: Inflation-adjusted by R-CPI-U-RS, not seasonally adjusted. CPI rent price index is the average rent of primary residences in U.S. cities.
Source: U.S. Bureau of Labor Statistics; S&P Dow Jones Indices; CPS; Treasury staff calculations.

While this may not be a complete explanation for the stress, it does validate the concern, and you may not have the flexibility to move to a lower cost location. Tristin Chambers, a 26-year-old e-sports streamer and entrepreneur, has lived through this transition and has gained some perspective. "Addressing these issues requires a re-evaluation of societal expectations and the creation of more affordable housing options."

I do want to pose an important question for you to consider: ***What's the difference between how much money you want versus how much you need?*** Living within your means is an option, and saving for later is also an important calculation. I'm not going to directly quote your parents here, but I bet you can guess their opinion on the topic.

Personally, I didn't have a full-time job with health benefits until eight years after I graduated college. I was 29 years old. It may sound strange, but freelance and consulting work are real options. Side hustles, gig economy, and flexible WFH (work from home) hours have opened the door to more options for putting your financial puzzle together.

One trend has definitely gained steam over the last two decades—living with your parents into your 20s and 30s. See the chart below that reflects data from the Census Bureau, allowing for an anomaly during the COVID-19 pandemic.

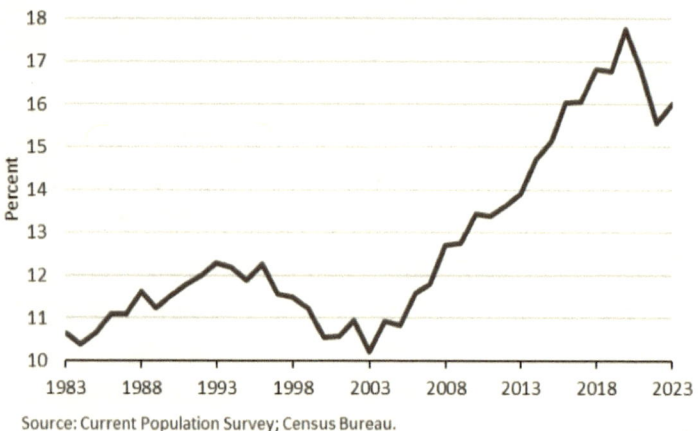

Source: Current Population Survey; Census Bureau.

I'm not fundamentally against this—it would be nice to spend more time with my kids, so maybe it is a temporary solution as you find your way that doesn't need to be a burden. According to a 22-year-old recent graduate, Jason in California: "Living at home is a stigma, but the financial relief is real."

According to the US Census, there are approximately 35 million people aged 18 to 25 in the US as of 2025 projections.[119] When researching this age group, it quickly became obvious that traditional timelines for leaving home and getting married have shifted dramatically. In fact, in 2023 more than 57 percent of people in your age group were living at home.[120] For some families, this is a cultural preference. But for many others, it is a symptom of a cohort of youth with fewer economic prospects and more emotional insecurities.

In Canada, men are more likely than women to be at home, partly because women tend to enter longer-term relationships earlier than men. Still, the rate of young adults who are in committed relationships and living as couples has been declining steadily, from over 68 percent 30 years ago, to just 45 percent today.[121]

Here are a few resources that you may find useful in managing your financial stress by increasing your financial knowledge:

- Money Skills for the Anxious Generation by Madison Blair
- Khan Academy Financial Literacy Course
- The College Investor (thecollegeinvestor.com)
- Gen Z for Financial Literacy (genzforfinlit.org)

Other graduates are even more pragmatic about career choice, realizing your **self worth is not determined by your net worth.** "I've never had a clear dream job; I want financial stability to support a family," said Henry, a

23-year-old college student in Texas.[122] Or Xoshil in San Francisco, "Sometimes, I agree with the narrative that your career is just a means of staying alive and having a roof over your head."[123]

Coaching Question: What financial trade-offs are worth sacrificing for your preferred career path?

CHAPTER 14
Religion, Faith and Spirituality

My faith helps me cope with stress and uncertainty about my future. I pray when I feel overwhelmed.
21-year-old female healthcare major,
Kissimmee, Florida

I partnered with a graduate school student last year who was having a really difficult time adapting to life in a new country: challenging classes, a job search, and some personal concerns. When I asked him what he usually does to calm his mind, he said he reads scripture in the morning and then goes for a walk in a peaceful location. I checked back in with him the following week and he had found some peace within himself and was better able to prioritize his worries and focus on the most important tasks ahead—those which he could control.

The diversity of faith definitions in our country is vast and important to appreciate. Whether it's a specific religion or liturgy, there's a spiritual element in many people's lives that is incredibly present for you and foundational to how you cope, how you make decisions, how you set goals, and how you think about your career in the context of a greater purpose.

This becomes even clearer as you leave your parents' house. On your own for the first time, it's up to you how you keep up cultural or religious traditions or habits. Your values may be tested at this time and experimentation is commonplace. **Part of growing up is deciding who you want to be, how you want to treat people, and the beliefs that you choose to embrace.**

This topic arose straight from my research interviews, and although it didn't come up in many of them, when it did—it sounded incredibly powerful. That shouldn't be a surprise, a Pew Research study from 2024 indicated that 57 percent of 18- to 24-year-olds claim a religious affiliation.[124] A separate study from the University of the Pacific even found that students with a strong connection to their faith generally experienced lower levels of anxiety, often finding relief through prayer and other spiritual practices.[125]

I'm not espousing a religion or proselytizing here, just relaying some data that may be helpful for some of you. This also isn't just about reading a Bible verse every morning. Respondents used terms such as faith, religion, and spirituality, and I am embracing all of those in this chapter.

Some put it on par with leaning on friends and participating in hobbies, and many see a higher purpose. Henry says, "My church has been the light at the end of the tunnel during tough times."

Nevaeh explains it like this, "I think that hope within my faith is what drives me to stay hopeful and know that in the end it will all work out."

Leaning on faith doesn't always provide complete clarity, according to a 22-year-old male business student in San Antonio. He says, "I sometimes feel torn between my religious values and the career choices my family wants me to make."

I honestly didn't expect to hear so much about religion when I started this project, but now I understand the situation better. For many of you, faith is fundamental to your daily experience. That especially includes times of need or when you want some help making big decisions. This is a very personal topic, so I will do my best to address it objectively and from your point of view.

Faith and Community

There's also an element of community engagement and support that can't be ignored. Jonathan Haidt writes in The Anxious Generation, "A phone-based life generally pulls people downward. It changes the way we think, feel, judge, and relate to others. It is incompatible with many of the behaviors that religious and spiritual communities practice, some of which have been shown to improve happiness, well-being, trust, and group cohesion."

The community element has been priceless for a 20-year-old college student from Chicago. "Being involved in my church community has given me mentors and support I couldn't find elsewhere."

My religious community has meant a lot to me, too. Growing up in a Jewish Sunday School, becoming a Bar Mitzvah, going to temple for High Holiday services and celebrating holidays has always been about family, friends, and the Jewish community at large. It's a wonder to think about so many people upholding similar traditions over thousands of years, across the world and close to home. Along the way, I learned important values such as *tikkun olam* (healing the world), and tzedakah (charity and justice). I also encountered important role models, some directly like our rabbis and religious school teachers.

Further afield, as a huge sports fan, I looked up to some famous Jewish athletes like Mark Spitz and Sandy Koufax. As it turned out, many of my colleagues and mentors in the media industry were also Jewish. When you find people at the office that you can relate to on another level, is that comforting for you, too?

Journalist Rikki Schlott wrote an article in *The New York Post* in May 2025 on the role of religion in the happiness of young people.[126] She quotes a few Gen Zers on the topic:

Sarah-Elisabeth Ellison said, "My faith has ebbed and flowed and changed a lot as I've grown up, but it's always been consistently there for me to fall back on."

Fay Dubinsky of Boca Raton, Florida, leans on Judaism for support. "I grew up Jewish and religious, and I think that's probably one of the reasons that I'm not depressed or anxious," she said.

For Alexander, Christianity helps him view his disability with a grounded perspective. "The fact that I'm still here 28 years later makes me believe that God has me here for a reason," he said. "The idea that I'm here for a purpose keeps me from falling into the generational nihilism."[127]

Spirituality is clearly a core consideration for people of all ages whether you worship at a church, temple, mosque, or in your own home. Prayer and meditation also seem to go hand-in-hand for a creative/design graduate in San Francisco who says, "I rely on meditation and spiritual practices to deal with anxiety about finding a job."

Practice Makes Progress

Personally, meditation has become one of my most valuable stress reduction practices. I have completed 100 hours of meditation since I was laid off a few years ago, and it has become a new superpower. Given the stress of corporate contraction, job searching, and ... life, I want to shed light on this very basic practice. My hope is that one of you might try meditation for the first time and find it improves your mindset at least one percent.

The benefits I've received to date are clear:

- I am less reactive later in the day and less likely to be triggered by potential stressors.
- I experience moments of clarity that help me make difficult decisions.
- Great ideas find their way into my consciousness.

To lower the bar on your potential participation, you should know that I meditate while walking my dog, Baxter, who you might remember from Chapter 4. I don't know if I'm doing it "right," but given the benefits I noted above, I think any method is okay. Everyone's meditation practice can be their own and I respect them all.

I also want to dispel some meditation myths that might answer some beginner questions:

- **Meditation does not have to be practiced in complete silence** to be valuable. I only use one AirPod so I can hear nature in the other ear, or an early morning driver approaching.

- **Meditation does not have to be practiced when sitting still** to be valuable.
- **Meditation does not have to be practiced for a long time every day** to be valuable. My usual session is 10 to 15 minutes, about five times per week.
- **Meditation does not make me perfect.** There's a reason it's called a practice.

Shout out to the Balance app from Elevate Labs which is my go-to home for my head. I have also heard positive reviews of the Calm and Peloton apps from others. Whatever works for you, I hope you try it soon. For what it's worth, I had a daily meditation reminder in my calendar for two years before I started. It took awhile to get going, but once I got going, I haven't been the same since.

Student Sanctuaries

One avenue I discovered during my coaching journey is the concept of a Career Ministry. Through my partnership with CMP (Career Management Partners), I was fortunate to meet Tracy Voegtle who leads such a group at All Saints Catholic Church in Dallas, Texas. As described on their website, "All Saints Career Ministry (ASCM) aims to provide counsel and training to those transitioning in their career, experiencing employment challenges, and/or looking to develop professionally. ASCM seeks to educate, equip, and encourage our community to hear God's calling and ensure that our participants are thriving in the right role."

Each summer the Career Ministry holds an event for young adults and college students focused on providing support, guidance and encouragement during this critical stage of life.

Tracy recently spearheaded one such event, entitled "Purpose & Planning for Career & College," where young professionals and students came together for free food and fellowship, inspiring talks and panel discussions, worship music, and small group connection. They also received access to a free career assessment. Keynote speaker and local CBS News Anchor Amelia Mugavero inspired the audience with these encouraging words, "You don't have to have it all figured out—just take the next best step in your own journey."

The foundation for many of the career ministries across the country has been provided by Crossroads Career, a faith-based non-profit organization that helps people hear God's calling, get the right job, and maximize their potential. If that's something that sounds like it might help you out, I encourage you to see if there's a chapter in your area, or you can download the available online resources.

In Atlanta, where I live, there's a very active branch of Jewish Family & Career Services that hosts job readiness workshops, provides career coaching and a variety of community resources for non-denominational job seekers of all ages.

I'm not going to list every faith-based career-related resource, but hopefully this gives you a sense of what is out there, and might be right for you. As I mentioned previously, being aware of support is just the first step. It's up to you to take advantage of the abundant resources around you.

Coaching Question: How might faith or spirituality help you manage stress during your career journey?

CHAPTER 15
World Events

World news is overwhelming and makes planning ahead feel impossible.

21-year-old female college student,
Los Angeles, CA

Do you ever avoid the news because it's just too depressing and you're not sure what to do about it? Another grown-up topic is how you decide to ingest and digest the news cycle. Over my last weeklong vacation, I took a diet from the news. A pause. A cleanse of sorts. No TV, no notifications, no social media. The mere fact that I needed to take a break was evidence enough that the world was depressing me. Too much hate, conflict, and strife. It hurts my heart, and daily doomscrolling only deepens the hurt. One of the reasons I think I'm a good career coach is my empathy. Hopefully some of that shows throughout this book.

One thing that became clear during the pandemic is that while I do feel the joy of others as an emotional high, I also dwell in others' suffering longer than most. That doesn't mean I want to turn a blind eye to reality, and I do desperately want to do something to help others, but sometimes I feel hopeless amid the grand scale and magnitude of the challenge.

From a macro standpoint, 49 percent of survey respondents cited "world events" (pandemic, climate change, politics) as contributing to their stress. Although it was over five years ago, the COVID-19 pandemic is still consistently referenced as disruptive to mental health, and several said the pandemic specifically impacted their career plans.

> *COVID changed everything—I lost my internship and my confidence.*
>
> 24-year-old female college graduate in New Orleans, Louisiana

There are plenty of reasons to be despondent and angry. War, climate, dictatorships, discrimination, religious persecution, social injustice, poverty, the list goes on ...

When the future of the world is unknown, young adults struggle more to grasp their own futures—on top of the stressors commonly associated with college and post college transitions.[128]

COVID-19 created a significant shift in expectation and motivation. Research on the mental health effects during the pandemic offer a glimpse of insight. We all had a ringside seat to our own mortality, or those around us.

What age were you during lockdown? How do you think it affected your personality, behavior, and career motivation?

In my previous book, I discussed how the COVID-19 pandemic and the social implications of it motivated me to seize the day, and I quietly began to consider professional options that felt more meaningful than my previous role. However, some days the death and destruction around us led me towards indifference.

So, what are your options for processing despair?

> 1. You can fall even deeper into depression and refuse to break out of your slump. This is honestly understandable, and on our worst days, it can happen to any of us. But prolonged negativity and isolation will not serve you well, or bring about the change your heart yearns for.
>
> 2. Ignore it all. That's a tough angle and might force you into an isolated bubble of self-serving ignorance

that might help in the short term, but it delays the inevitable onslaught of reality.

3. Do something. Anything. The Mayo Clinic has found that volunteer service has been shown to reduce stress and increase positive, relaxed feelings by releasing dopamine.[129]

So, you can exhibit small acts of kindness every day, or you could even turn this personal passion into a genuine career pursuit. A purpose. A mission. That may sound daunting or not feel like something you can accomplish, but any baby steps could make you feel better and put you on a better path. In 2022, over 300,000 nonprofit establishments accounted for 12.8 million jobs, or 9.9 percent of all private-sector jobs.[130]

Everything ranging from arts to education to international affairs is open to you, and there are jobs in the nonprofit world for the same functions as exist in corporate America—accounting, analytics, communications, marketing, etc. Yes, in most cases, wages are lower in this sector, but that's a trade-off—you can decide if it's a worthwhile exchange for yourself.

What causes and issues drive you? What charities have you been involved with in the past? In some cases, that might mean a compromise on income, but that's not true in all cases, and the trade-off could be life changing. It may not be a panacea, but **waking up most days with**

hope and purpose might be the priceless option you've been looking for.

Have you ever heard the song, *We Didn't Start the Fire*, by Fall Out Boy? It was released in 2023 and preceded by the original version performed by Billy Joel in 1995. The lyrics are similar, but different. Cold War turned into Culture Wars. Mentions of TV celebrities were replaced by social influencers. Issues in North Korea, Afghanistan, and Lebanon even bridge both worlds.

Sadly, as I have been in the process of writing this book over several months, bad things continue to happen to good people. It's a lot to take, but we're all in it together, and I hope you take care of yourself and treat others with grace and kindness. We all have bad days, and sometimes a smile in the hallway or a quick hug might be just what you need.

The problems of each generation evolve, but what I think is different in this era is the social media proliferation. The sights and sounds of injustice can really feel overwhelming. For babies born after 2000, 21st Century stress is a viral beast.

Even so, I hope you realize that you didn't start the wars, you didn't create famine ... some of you haven't even voted yet. You don't have to feel the pressure to solve all world problems, but you can do something. Volunteer. Help a cause you believe in. Demonstrate kindness one person at a time. **I hope you choose support over scorn, love over hate, hugs over hubris, empathy over evil, caring over killing.** You get the idea. Are you even more ambitious? Then find a way to lead others into the light. You never know what ripple effect you might create.

Coaching Question: How much does your news consumption affect your mood?

CHAPTER 16
Entrepreneurship

I want to be part of a startup where my work has meaning and purpose.

Max, 22-year-old Indiana business school graduate[131]

There are so many great things about being an entrepreneur. The sheer freedom of deciding what you want to do, not having to listen to other people, and believing anything is possible. It might seem like you won't ever have to depend on anyone else. However, the challenge with being an entrepreneur is that none of that is actually true, especially if you want to be successful. As the African proverb says: "If you want to go fast, go alone. If you want to go far, go together." I'm not here to dissuade you from being entrepreneurial, but I want you to be aware of the trade-offs.

The truth is that **startups have never been more popular or possible with young professionals** than they are now. I've had high school interns who had already built and sold multiple companies. Barriers to entry are lower than ever. If you want to launch an app, go for it. Interested in starting a social media influencer career? Nothing is stopping you. There are plenty of businesses that have minimal fixed costs, but at some point, you might need capital—that means raising money from other people. Those people become your investors, and they usually have a voice in what you are doing.

Alright, let's say that's not an issue ... then, the next occasion you may need some help is in building and running your business. Again, maybe with technology, you can harness extremely efficient solutions that you oversee from the luxury of your laptop on a Caribbean island. But if you can do it, can't somebody else? What resources and skills do your competitors have access to? How will that impact your scalability? I realize this is sounding like a wet blanket.

When I spoke to my friend Misha Leybovich about this conundrum, I was inspired. He's a serial entrepreneur and has also spent time working as an executive at SpaceX and in Google's AI division. Here's how he put it simply,

"The person with the best idea can win, if executed the best. AI capabilities lower the barrier to participation, where anyone can now test their best ideas, and iterate until they really work." Further discussion led us to agree that you still need to apply a strategic filter and follow through in order to select and execute on the right idea at the right time.[132]

As I first started my coaching business, one of the first organizations I partnered with was the Emory Hatchery Innovation Center, led by my friend Shannon Clute. For two nights in a row, I met with a dozen students who had startup ideas they were pursuing, and I coached them through the various challenges they were facing—ideation, market sizing, operationalizing, etc. The concepts ranged from fast fashion, to an audacious cancer cure, to a political analytics platform. It was an exhilarating experience, hearing their hopes, plans, dreams, and visions for commercialization, and for developing solutions to create a better society. Ah, the idealism of youth. I loved it.

It was truly a glimpse into a common trend, as Babson University's Global Entrepreneurship Monitor (GEM) report found that 20 percent of 18- to 24-year-olds had high entrepreneurial intentions."[133] A 20-year-old student from Miami says, "I want to be my own boss someday— maybe open a gym or a sports clinic."

And before you downplay the potential, there are investors who sing your praises. Tristin Chambers is a 15x founder and owner of an e-sports team. He says "16- to 25-year-olds are often undervalued due to their age, but they are among the smartest and hardest working individuals."

New Dreams for a New Generation

According to a 2024 survey of 12- to 15-year-olds by Whop, a marketplace for creators to sell various digital products, **Gen Alpha's top career choice is to become a YouTuber or TikToker.**[134] "They've grown up watching influencers make millions from daily vlogs and video game content—now they want a piece of the pie," according to a *Fortune Magazine* article by Emma Burleigh. For what it's worth, here are the top 10 most desired jobs of the next generation[135]:

- YouTuber (32 percent)
- TikTok creator (21 percent)
- Doctor/nurse (20 percent)
- Mobile app/video game developer (19 percent)
- Entrepreneur (17 percent)
- Artist (16 percent)
- Sports athlete (15 percent)
- Professional online streamer (15 percent)
- Musician (14 percent)
- Teacher (14 percent)

Remember the client I mentioned in chapter five who has created a portfolio career out of a variety of puzzle pieces? She was the one who inspired the "Found" scale. Part of her finding herself was realizing that she was an entrepreneur at heart, inspired by her parents, and she has proven capable at every turn. She just needed the knowledge, courage and support to go after it, and now she's earning revenue as a social media consultant, with real estate income alongside her main gig.

However, even though you have a dream of running a company, you also have some concerns like these:

> *I want to start my own business, but I don't know where to begin. No one in my family has done it before.*
>
> 23-year-old male with a business degree from Cleveland, Ohio

> *Entrepreneurship seems exciting, but I'm worried about the risk and if I can make enough money to live.*
>
> 21-year-old female college student from Los Angeles, California

> *"I've thought about launching a creative studio, but I don't have a mentor who has started a business.*
>
> 22-year-old nonbinary college student from San Francisco, California

> *My dream is to build a tech company, but it feels out of reach without connections or funding.*
>
> 21-year-old male engineering major in Austin, Texas

I'm interested in entrepreneurship, but college doesn't really teach you how to do it.
    22-year-old female business graduate,
    Chicago, Illinois

The Builder's Toolkit

If you're on a college campus, there may be startup resources available like Emory's Hatchery. Or, you might find some role models to follow on LinkedIn, such as Brianna Doe who transparently shares her favorite tools for launching and operating a small business[136]:

- Websites (Personal + Agency): Webflow
- Contracting: PandaDoc
- Presentations & Pitch Decks: Pitch
- Invoicing: Anchor (Absolute game changer, I highly recommend. Easy to use and they only charge $5/payment received.)
- Analytics: Aware
- Invoicing: BILL
- Podcast Recording: Streamyard
- Podcast Production & Editing: Shoutout to the GURU Media Hub team for this. I couldn't (and wouldn't) do this without y'all.

In today's challenging job market, full-time roles and long-term company stability can seem like an illusion. In fact, the risk profile of an entrepreneurial option may not be as different as it once was. And, that path comes with potentially powerful trade-offs such as flexibility and control. By no means is launching a new company a guaranteed success, but **would you rather be a cog in a corporation or bet on yourself?** I've had a lot of clients recently choosing the latter.

Ready, Set, Go!

This is a startup launch process in an era of uncertainty ...

After two decades in a great job, I found myself at a crossroads—freshly laid off and energized by the idea of starting my own business. That's when I created my "Ready, Set, Go" methodology—for myself, and for others who want to launch their own business. Simple in name and populated with only the most critical steps, this helped fuel an action bias that avoided my tendency towards analysis paralysis.

Here's how I navigated launching my own business, Doyne Services, LLC:

Ready: I will always start with research, but I also have to know when I have "enough" to move forward. Another healthy reminder that done is better than perfect. But I did talk to 30 coaches, I did analyze the types of coaching in the market. I did review a key ICF (International Coaching Federation) study on the future of coaching. With these initial insights in hand, the remainder of the ready stage was about vision and intention. I started by clarifying what I wanted—autonomy, flexibility, control, and maximum impact. I dug deep into my goals, both for my family and for the business. I also drafted a mission that meant something: Equitable access to career fulfillment through individual engagement. This stage was about defining my "why" and laying the foundation for everything to come.

Set: Here's where the rubber met the road. I tackled the logistics: forming the LLC, opening a business banking account, building a draft of my brand and my coaching toolkit. But "Set" was more than paperwork—I also assembled an informal board of advisors: accountant, attorney, executive coach, HR pro, and a "Voice of the Customer." I had to embrace imperfection and get comfortable with the MVP (Minimum Viable Product) mindset. Pre-launch coaching practice and feedback from trusted peers gave me the confidence to move forward, even without a polished logo or website.

Go! Launch day arrived—March 1, 2023. I hit "post" on LinkedIn, shared my story, and invited my network to join me on this new journey. I leaned into experimentation, measurement, and adaptation—principles that also served me well in corporate life. My first offers were simple: complimentary consultations and straightforward coaching packages for all stages of career transition. The learning hasn't stopped since.

If you're considering your own leap into entrepreneurship, here are a few highlights to keep in mind:

- Start with your purpose
- Build your support system
- Launch before you feel "ready"

The real growth happens once you're already in motion. Best wishes on defining and achieving your dreams!

Coaching Question: If you could launch any business, who would be your ideal partner?

Section 6

Coaching

CHAPTER 17
What is Coaching?

It's like career therapy—asking questions that unlock your creativity, helping you explore diverse possibilities, and equipping you with the tools to turn those ideas into reality.

Confidential coaching client

As a certified professional career coach, I don't want you to close this book without getting a sense of the benefits of the practice I have come to respect so much. Hopefully, you've absorbed some of the value throughout the book, as portrayed in some client success stories. I'll tell you more about coaching in a second, but first I'll share some reflections from my younger clients:

Always in my corner, nonjudgmental support.

Thoughtful, personalized guidance beyond sessions.

No pressure—respects my pace of career exploration.

Caring professionalism and a genuine desire to help.

Validates my passions and acknowledges my strengths.

Tracks progress and encourages innovative thinking.

Holistic approach that considers emotional and cultural factors.

Relieves stress and helps me organize my next steps.

Does this type of support sound valuable to you? This may seem impressive, but I promise, what I do pales in comparison to some master coaches out there and even a lot of the coaches in your college career or alumni office.

So, what is coaching?

If you're a sports fan, you might think I'm talking about Dawn Staley, Pep Guardiola or Zac Taylor. (Yes, I'm a proud Cincinnati Bengals fan). While I did enjoy coaching my kids' little league teams, this is not that kind of coaching.

The International Coaching Federation (ICF) defines professional coaching as, "partnering with clients in a thought-provoking and creative process that inspires them to maximize their personal and professional potential."

Why does coaching work?

Again from the ICF, "The process of coaching often unlocks previously untapped sources of imagination, productivity, and leadership."

Here's a piece of recent client feedback that is representative of the method and results.

> *I really enjoyed the session and appreciated the opportunity to just brain dump a bit. Scott was clearly listening, which helped me crystallize my thoughts and have a better sense of what I am looking for in my career.*

What happens in a coaching session?

Here's how the sessions usually work, leaving plenty of room for growth:

A critical key to the process is that I, as a coach, will not tell you what to do. I will ask questions, I will listen, I will take notes, I will draw diagrams, I will ask more questions … as Erickson teaches, I will use art and science to guide you through a variety of exercises to help you identify potential solutions and an action plan that you believe you can achieve. As said by Marilyn Atkinson, founder of

Erickson Coaching International, "Coaches help people discover and live their true purpose."[137]

You will be thoughtful, introspective, open to your own new ideas, and ultimately accountable. Most importantly, we will make progress together.

Prominent Coach and Author Rich Litvin said on the Marisa Peer podcast, *Master Your Mind with Marisa*, "Coaching is helping people I'm with see possibilities that they can't see from the direction they're looking at in this moment in time."[138]

One last quote from another famous coach, "Success is not about the wins and losses. It's about helping these young fellas be the best versions of themselves on and off the field." Ted Lasso, AFC Richmond

So maybe these different kinds of coaches do have something in common.

If you're interested in meeting a coach who will have your best interests in mind, I'd recommend searching the ICF website for certified coaches. Most will have a free intro session available for new customers. I'd also suggest checking out Pay Forward Coaching (PFC). This is an organization that offers free sessions from a volunteer base of qualified coaches.

Mike Connolly is the CEO of PFC and provides these encouraging words for anyone having a difficult time in the job hunt: "We talk to incredibly talented people every day who have applied to hundreds of jobs, and they're doing all the right things. It's just the reality of where we are now. It's not you—and it is solvable. You can still launch and advance your career successfully."[139]

Coaching Question: What would you want from an ideal partner in your career journey?

Conclusion

I'd like you to end your experience with this book where we started in the Introduction, with a deep breath.

Alright ... take a moment ... *to breathe.*

I hope the words from your contemporaries on the previous pages unlocked something novel and mighty in your life—newfound comfort with uncertainty, contentment with change, perhaps a light at the end of the tunnel.

If you've made it this far, thank you. And thank yourself. You've invested time and energy into deconstructing your early career challenges. Bravo. It is not necessary to immediately implement every suggestion or idea from this book, but what I will ask you to do is think for a moment about what you have learned—about yourself, about the world, about your peers. I hope what you've discovered is that you are not alone. Most 18- to 25-year-olds are struggling with where they are, what they are doing, and how well things are going (or not).

Whatever you are seeing on social media about ultimate joy and riches is largely a farce. Your journey will be long, squiggly and bumpy. I hope you can accept that reality, not with depression, but in recognition that your life will be richer as a result. Struggle builds character. Setbacks lead to comebacks. **True happiness can be the outcome of trial, tribulation and triumph.** So, you don't have to hope for shortcuts, but you can still take pride and pleasure in the successes along the way.

Naveah is now approaching graduation and trying to take a realistic approach to going with the flow, "It's just a matter of leaning with the pivots and going with it, not trying to force something that's not gonna be there. If a door shuts, it shut for a reason."

Another client is still in her first job post-graduation with Arista Records. She isn't loving it, but she's trying to be optimistic about her situation: "I am a firm believer that everything happens for a reason. I do think things will work out, so I just keep trying to remind myself of that. And I try to remind myself that a lot of other people are in my position, as well."

Jack is finding hope in his new role, "For this job, it really does feel like the sky is the limit. I feel empowered to take my ideas, no matter how lofty, and run with them."

In the meantime, as Simone says, "You have to give yourself grace and pat yourself on the back when you have those little wins. You can't get anywhere big without making little leaps." Coincidentally, Simone just found out that little wins do lead to big wins. She told me this week that she's on her way to Charleston, South Carolina, as the newest reporter for a local TV station.

A few months ago, Naomi was still in the job search grind. She said at the time, "What gives me hope is that every day I always look for new jobs, and there is stuff available. It may not be entry level. It may not be exactly what I want, but I still apply to it, because there's a chance that people will get back to me." Less than a year since she submitted one of those applications, she's moved to Charlotte, North Carolina, and is happily working in the exact role she was hoping for. She even asked her father recently, "Is work supposed to be this fun?"

I still get chills when I think about that journey. At times, all you can see are the roadblocks, the detours, everyone else succeeding ahead of you, the countless rejections and ghostings. But, it doesn't have to be scary. It will work out. You can do this.

And ... *exhale* ...

If you or someone you know are struggling with severe anxiety, please reach out for support. Help is available. You can call or text 988 or chat 988lifeline. org to reach the 988 Crisis Lifeline.

Acknowledgments

I'd like to start by thanking the people who were instrumental in supporting me during my own Quarterlife stage:

My parents, brother, in-laws, friends and especially my wife, Aimee, who I was so fortunate to find during college and I've cherished our partnership ever since. I love you all.

My mentors, teachers, classmates, and advisors at The University of Michigan and Emory University's Goizueta Business School. You supported and shaped me in ways impossible to articulate.

I'd also like to thank the younger generations of employees, interns, students, coachees, and mentees who trusted me and guided me towards a passion for helping young professionals achieve their career and life goals.

Related to the writing, editing, publishing and research phase of this book, I am forever indebted to the following contributors:

> Everyone I interviewed for the book who provided vulnerable and powerful perspectives on Quarterlife, and specific ideas and resources that will help future generations.
>
> The Ripples Media Publishing community of authors, leaders and editors, including Jeff Hilimire, Andrew Vogel, Nicole Wedekind, Alexa Cole, Kathy Sindorf, Joe Sindorf, Carolyn Asman and Dorothy Miller-Farleo. Your partnership during the entire process has been priceless, and any impact our work makes on the world will be a shared accomplishment.
>
> To Rennie Curran, for contributing a heartfelt and inspiring Foreword. You are an incomparable champion with an outsized ability to help us all be better versions of ourselves.

Lastly, I want to thank the readers of this book for bravely embracing the challenges of Quarterlife and doing what you can to emerge with character, grace and joy.

Endnotes

1   Haleigh (interview with author, May 2, 2025).

2   Centers for Disease Control and Prevention. "Mortality in the United States, 2023." NCHS Data Brief No. 521. Centers for Disease Control and Prevention, May 2024. https://www.cdc.gov/nchs/products/databriefs/db521.htm.

3   Nevaeh (interview with author, April 28, 2025).

4   Scott Doyne, Career Survey: Analysis of 18–25-Year-Olds (proprietary study, May 2025).

5   Gusto. "New Grad Hiring Report 2025." Gusto. May 21, 2024. https://gusto.com/company-news/new-grad-hiring-report-2025.

6   Susan Svrluga, "Class of 2025 Say Market, Student Loan Debt Impact Their Career Plans," Inside Higher Ed, August 22, 2024, https://www.insidehighered.com/news/student-success/life-after-college/2024/08/22/class-2025-say-market-student-loan-debt-impact.

7   University of Phoenix. "The Impact of Generative AI on the Future of Work: A University of Phoenix® White Paper." University of Phoenix, October 2023. https://www.phoenix.edu/content/dam/edu/media-center/doc/whitepapers/genai-report-final-remediated.pdf.

8   Tallo. "The Resource Gap: How to Close the Divide Between Students and Opportunity." Tallo, October 26, 2023. https://tallo.com/the-resource-gap/.

9   LinkedIn News, "New LinkedIn Research Shows 75 Percent of 25-33 Year-Olds Have Either Quit or Are Considering Quitting Their Jobs Because of a Lack of Learning and Development Opportunities," LinkedIn News, November 15, 2017, https://news.linkedin.com/2017/11/new-linkedin-research-shows-75-percent-of-25-33-year-olds-have-e.

10   Substance Abuse and Mental Health Services Administration. "2022 National Survey of Drug Use and Health: National Report." Rockville, MD: Substance Abuse and Mental Health Services Administration, 2023. https://www.samhsa.gov/data/sites/default/files/reports/rpt42731/2022-nsduh-nnr.pdf.

11   Healthy Minds Network, "Healthy Minds Study National Report 2022–2023," August 2023, https://healthymindsnetwork.org/wp-content/uploads/2023/08/HMS_National-Report-2022-2023_full.pdf.

12   Substance Abuse and Mental Health Services Administration, "Key Substance Use and Mental Health Indicators in the United States: Results from the 2020 National Survey on Drug Use and Health," HHS Publication No. PEP21-07-01-007, NSDUH Series H-56 (Rockville, MD: Substance Abuse and Mental Health Services Administration, 2021), https://www.samhsa.gov/data/sites/default/files/reports/rpt35325/NSDUHFFRPDFWHTMLFiles2020/2020NSDUHFFR1PDFW102121.pdf.

13 Doyne, Career Survey.

14 William (interview with author, April 21, 2025).

15 Alfred, Lord Tennyson, "In Memoriam A.H.H.," in The Poetical Works of Alfred, Lord Tennyson: Complete Edition From the Author's Text, With Numerous Illustrations by English and American Artists (Boston: Houghton, Mifflin and Company, 1885), section 27, line 4.

16 Positive Intelligence. "Saboteurs." Accessed November 2, 2025. https://www.positiveintelligence.com/saboteurs/.

17 Theodore Roosevelt, "Citizenship in a Republic" (address delivered at the Sorbonne, Paris, April 23, 1910).

18 "Denzel Washington has finally found his purpose (it's not acting)." Penn Today, February 8, 2025. https://penntoday.upenn.edu/penn-in-the-news/denzel-washington-has-finally-found-his-purpose-its-not-acting.

19 "Taylor Swift's NYU Commencement Speech: Read the Full Transcript," Billboard, May 18, 2022, https://www.billboard.com/music/music-news/taylor-swift-nyu-commencement-speech-full-transcript-1235072824/

20 "The video store that turned Quentin Tarantino into a director," BBC News, October 11, 2024, https://www.bbc.com/articles/c4g40ndzpe0o

21 Phil Hoad, "Kevin Smith: how we made Clerks," The Guardian, May 7, 2019, https://www.theguardian.com/film/2019/may/07/how-we-made-clerks-kevin-smith

22 Lena Finkel, "How Donald Glover Got His Job at '30 Rock'," Femestella, accessed November 7, 2025, https://www.femestella.com/donald-glover-30-rock/

23 Ana Isaacson, "How Judd Apatow Started Preparing for His Career at 10 Years Old," CNBC, August 5, 2017, https://www.cnbc.com/2017/08/05/how-judd-apatow-started-preparing-for-his-career-at-10-years-old.html

24 Ryan Holiday, The Obstacle Is the Way: The Timeless Art of Turning Trials into Triumph (New York: Portfolio/Penguin, 2014).

25 Liu, Katty. "Forget About Your Career Path. Embrace a Career Stumble." Helpful.com on Medium. October 27, 2023. https://medium.com/helpful-com/forget-about-your-career-path-embrace-a-career-stumble-helpful-7d71d0f4ef7b.

26 John Hartz, Failureship (Self-published: John Hartz, 2023).

27 Organisation for Economic Co-operation and Development, *Teenage Career Uncertainty: Why It Matters and How to Reduce It? (OECD Education Spotlights, No. 16, Paris: OECD Publishing, 2024), doi:10.1787/e89c3da9-en

28 Bounouh, Sarra. "The 70% rule that changed how I make every decision." LinkedIn post, June 7, 2025. https://www.linkedin.com/posts/sarrabounouh_the-70-rule-that-changed-how-i-make-every-activity-7303632203782008832-f-uk/.

29   Caroline, Castrillon. "Why Non-Linear Careers Are the Future of Work." Forbes, March 18, 2025. https://www.forbes.com/sites/carolinecastrillon/2025/03/18/why-non-linear-careers-are-the-future-of-work/.

30   Garrett (interview with author, June 3, 2025).

31   Helen Tupper and Sarah Ellis, Squiggly Career: Ditch the Ladder, Discover Opportunity, Design Your Career (New York: Portfolio/Penguin, 2020).

32   Kerns, Kitric. "My Professional Journey is a Jungle Gym, OK?" LinkedIn Pulse, February 21, 2024. https://www.linkedin.com/pulse/my-professional-journey-jungle-gym-ok-kitric-kerns-ly59c/.

33   Jack (interview with Alexa Cole, May 5, 2025).

34   Benwell, Max. "NEETs: What Do They Do?" Vice, February 7, 2017. https://www.vice.com/en/article/neets-what-do-they-do/.

35   Robinson, Bryan, Ph.D. "Micro-Retirement: The New Career Trend Rising Among Gen Z." Forbes, January 29, 2025. https://www.forbes.com/sites/bryanrobinson/2025/01/29/micro-retirement-the-new-career-trend-rising-among-gen-z/.

36   Meg Jay, The Defining Decade: Why Your Twenties Matter—And How to Make the Most of Them Now (New York: Twelve, 2012).

37   Cydney (interview with Scott, April 29, 2025).

38   Doyne, Career Survey.

39   Cortes, Michelle Santiago. "How Social Interactions Can Lower Your Cortisol." Vogue, October 18, 2023. https://www.vogue.com/article/social-interactions-lower-cortisol.

40   John Hartz, Unworried (Self-published: John Hartz, 2020).

41   Psychology Today. "Mark Cooperberg, MSW, LCSW." Accessed November 2, 2025. https://www.psychologytoday.com/us/therapists/mark-cooperberg-princeton-nj/261878.

42   Alexa (interview with author, April 17, 2025).

43   Cate LeSourd (interview with author, September 11, 2025).

44   Substance Abuse and Mental Health Services Administration (SAMHSA). Key Substance Use and Mental Health Indicators in the United States: Results from the 2022 National Survey on Drug Use and Health. Rockville, MD: Center for Behavioral Health Statistics and Quality, 2022. https://www.samhsa.gov/data/sites/default/files/reports/rpt42731/2022-nsduh-nnr.pdf.

45   Winerman, Lea. "Stress in America: Generation Z." Monitor on Psychology 50, no. 1 (January 2019). https://www.apa.org/monitor/2019/01/gen-z.

46   Pacific Oaks College. "Marriage and Family Therapy Programs." Accessed November 2, 2025. https://www.pacificoaks.edu/marriage-and-family-therapy-programs/.

47 Smith, Brandon. "How to Boost Your Workplace Happiness: Brandon Smith Posted on the Topic." LinkedIn, August 17, 2025. https://www.linkedin.com/posts/brandonsmithtwpt_are-you-unhappy-at-work-and-contemplating-activity-7362944167875887105-7zUs/.

48 David Yeager, 10 to 25: The Science of Motivating Young People (New York: Scribner, 2024).

49 Caydence (interview with author, April 21, 2025).

50 Simone (interview with Alexa Cole, May 1, 2025).

51 Doyne, Career Survey.

52 Tristin (interview with author, June 5, 2025).

53 "Transcript of Speech by President Barack Obama." Transcript of Speech by President Barack Obama | Barnard College, May 12, 2012. https://barnard.edu/commencement/archives/2012/barack-obama-remarks.

54 Stacey Young Rivers, Career Smarts for College Students: A Practical Career Guide for Work in the Age of AI (Self-published, 2023).

55 Parul Khosla (interview with author, August 20, 2025). Doyne, Career Survey.

56 Evans, Dave, and Bill Burnett. Designing your life. Penguin Random House Audio Publishing Group, 2016.

57 Jonathan Haidt, Anxious Generation: How the Great Rewiring of Childhood Is Causing an Epidemic of Mental Illness (New York: Penguin Press, 2024).

58 Burick, Jordan. @leveragedbyclout. "How I got my first investment banking Super Day." Instagram post, October 24, 2024. https://www.instagram.com/p/DEXiIt-FRcbG/.

59 Oguneye, Olaoluwa. "I'm about to let you in on one of the best growth hacks for early-stage career professionals..." LinkedIn post, October 26, 2025. https://www.linkedin.com/posts/olaoluwa-oguneye_im-about-to-let-you-in-on-one-of-the-best-ugcPost-7357526499568066561-orV9.

60 Megan Cerullo, "Rising number of college grads are unemployed, new research shows," CBS News, August 4, 2017, https://www.cbsnews.com/news/college-graduate-unemployed-technology-artificial-intelligence/

61 Lucas Mearian, "Tech hiring slows, unemployment rises, jobs report shows," Computerworld, May 3, 2025, https://www.computerworld.com/article/3976643/tech-hiring-slows-unemployment-rises-jobs-report-shows.html

62 Connley, Courtney. "2 in 3 college seniors are stressed about the tight job market. Here's how to navigate it." CNBC, August 21, 2024. https://www.cnbc.com/2024/08/21/2-in-3-college-seniors-are-stressed-about-the-tight-job-market.html.

63 Handshake. "Class of 2025 Career Outlook Report." 2025. https://joinhandshake.com/network-trends/class-of-2025-career-outlook-report/.

64   Hirsch, Lauren, Sarah Kessler, and Eshe Nelson. "The White-Collar Layoffs Are Different This Time." The New York Times, March 25, 2025. https://www.nytimes.com/2025/03/25/business/economy/white-collar-layoffs.html.

65   National Association of Colleges and Employers (NACE). "More Than 70 Percent of Organizations Expect to Increase or Maintain Intern Hiring Despite Overall Dip in Hiring." March 6, 2024. https://www.naceweb.org/talent-acquisition/internships/more-than-70-percent-of-organizations-expect-to-increase-or-maintain-intern-hiring-despite-overall-dip-in-hiring.

66   LinkedIn News. "Who's struggling most with their employment?" LinkedIn post, July 29, 2025. https://www.linkedin.com/posts/linkedin-news_whos-struggling-most-with-their-employment-activity-7323713456933605377-lPGt/.

67   National Association of Colleges and Employers (NACE). "More Than 70 Percentof Organizations Expect to Increase or Maintain Intern Hiring Despite Overall Dip in Hiring." March 6, 2024. https://www.naceweb.org/talent-acquisition/internships/more-than-70-percent-of-organizations-expect-to-increase-or-maintain-intern-hiring-despite-overall-dip-in-hiring.

68   Urban Land Institute (ULI). "For Students." Accessed November 2, 2025. https://americas.uli.org/programs/learning/university-connections/for-students/.

69   Albrecht, Adam. What does your fortune cookie say?: 80 important life lessons the universe is trying to share with you. United States? Ripples Media, 2021.

70   Parker Dewey. "About." Accessed November 2, 2025. https://www.parkerdewey.com/about.

71   Fain, Paul. "Survey: What College Students Want in Career Services." Inside Higher Ed, November 30, 2023. https://www.insidehighered.com/news/student-success/life-after-college/2023/11/30/survey-what-college-students-want-career.

72   Doyne, Career Survey.

73   Tyton Partners. "Inside Higher Ed: Lack of Awareness Causes Students to Fall Through the Cracks." November 30, 2023. https://tytonpartners.com/inside-higher-ed-lack-of-awareness-causes-students-to-fall-through-the-cracks/.

74   National Association of Colleges and Employers (NACE). "The Value of Career Services." January 23, 2024. https://www.naceweb.org/career-development/organizational-structure/the-value-of-career-services/.

75   Joe Fiveash (interview with author, June 9, 2025).

76   Ben Moore (interview with author, July 24, 2025).

77   Jessica Santana (interview with author, August 27, 2025).

78   Mayer, Beth Ann. "What Parents Should Know about the Slow Job Market for New Grads." Parents, June 6, 2025. https://www.parents.com/recent-college-grads-struggling-find-work-what-parents-can-do-11748253.

79   News, and Lily Cooper. "115 Years Later: How Northeastern's Co-Op Program Grew with the University." The Huntington News, January 9, 2025. https://huntnewsnu.com/82523/campus/115-years-later-how-northeasterns-co-op-program-grew-with-the-university/.

80   Kern, Jacqueline. "Co-Op's $88 Million Impact." UC News, August 13, 2024. https://www.uc.edu/news/articles/2024/07/co-op-2024.html.

81   Davis, Anthony S. "Georgia State University is ensuring tomorrow's workforce is career ready." SaportaReport, November 15, 2023. https://saportareport.com/georgia-state-university-is-ensuring-tomorrows-workforce-is-career-ready/thought-leadership/higher-education/georgia-state-university/.

82   Marcus, Jon. "For new grads, landing a job may be hard, navigating the workplace may be harder." The Hechinger Report, October 25, 2023. https://hechingerreport.org/for-new-grads-landing-a-job-may-be-hard-navigating-the-workplace-may-be-harder/

83   Kim, Jeoungmi, Jina Oh, and Vasuki Rajaguru. "Job-Seeking Anxiety and Job Preparation Behavior of Undergraduate Students." Healthcare (Basel, Switzerland), February 1, 2022. https://pmc.ncbi.nlm.nih.gov/articles/PMC8872297/.

84   Marnie (interview with author, May 1, 2025).

85   Christina Alejandre (interview with author, August 20, 2025).

86   Leslie and Libby Marx (interview with author, September 4, 2025).

87   Job Corps. Accessed November 2, 2025. https://www.jobcorps.gov/.

88   Harvard Summer School. "Need a Break from Social Media? Here's Why You Should and How to Do It." Harvard Summer School Blog, May 17, 2023. https://summer.harvard.edu/blog/need-a-break-from-social-media-heres-why-you-should-and-how-to-do-it/.

89   Perez, Evelyn. "LinkedIn Might Be the Worst Social Media App for Gen Z." Vice, October 26, 2023. https://www.vice.com/en/article/linkedin-might-be-the-worst-social-media-app-for-gen-z/.

90   Inglehart, Ronald. "The Happiness of the Younger, the Older, and Those in Between." In World Happiness Report 2024. New York: Sustainable Development Solutions Network, 2024. https://www.worldhappiness.report/ed/2024/happiness-of-the-younger-the-older-and-those-in-between/.

91   Kanuri, Hannah. "Gen Z is more depressed than ever—but these Zoomers reveal their secrets to staying happy." New York Post, May 26, 2025. https://nypost.com/2025/05/26/lifestyle/gen-z-is-more-depressed-than-ever-but-these-zoomers-reveal-their-secrets-to-staying-happy/.

92   Smith, Ray A. "Gen Z Gets Career Advice, One TikTok at a Time." The Wall Street Journal, May 20, 2021. https://www.wsj.com/articles/gen-z-gets-career-advice-one-tiktok-at-a-time-11621526403.

93   Nicolette (interview with author, June 16, 2025).

94   Afrotech Staff. "Yale University Students Raised $3.1M In 14 Days To Launch A $10M Fund To Invest In Black And Latino Founders." Afrotech, October 26, 2023. https://afrotech.com/yale-university-students-raised-3-1m-in-14-days.

95   LinkedIn News. "Fastest-growing jobs: AI and frontline roles." LinkedIn post, December 19, 2024. https://www.linkedin.com/posts/linkedin-news_fastest-growing-jobs-ai-and-frontline-roles-activity-7282448785392246784-8DWq/.

96   LinkedIn News, "Fastest-growing jobs."

97   Jocelyne Gafner, "Report: 51% of Gen Z Views Their College Degree as a Waste of Money," Indeed Career Guide, May 7, 2025, https://www.indeed.com/career-advice/news/college-degree-value-generational-divide

98   Case, Garth. "An excellent slide that clearly articulates the shift in mindset required to build a thriving AI culture." LinkedIn post, September 3, 2025. https://www.linkedin.com/posts/garth-case-pluglabs-ai_ai-futureofwork-leadership-activity-7337175994153254912-K3eh/.

99   Liu, "As Many as 41% of Employers of Employers Plan to Use AI to Replace Roles.

100   Stacey Young Rivers, Career Smarts for College Students: A Practical Career Guide for Work in the Age of AI (Place of publication not specified: Self-published, 2023).

101   "The Future of Jobs Report 2025." World Economic Forum, January 7, 2025. https://www.weforum.org/publications/the-future-of-jobs-report-2025/in-full/3-skills-outlook/.

102   Ken Taylor (email message to author, October 29, 2025)

103   Levy, Steven. "No, Graduates: Ai Hasn't Ended Your Career before It Starts." Wired, May 16, 2025. https://www.wired.com/story/plaintext-commencement-speech-artificial-intelligence/.

104   Alexandra Robbins and Abby Wilner, Quarterlife Crisis: The Unique Challenges of Life in Your Twenties (New York: Tarcher/Putnam, 2001).

105   Life & Health. "Nearly Half of Young Americans Experienced a 'Quarter-Life Crisis.'" Accessed November 5, 2025. https://www.lifehealth.com/nearly-half-young-americans-experienced-quarter-life-crisis/.

106   Ashton (interview with author, April 30, 2025).

107   Tingley, Susan. "Two Key Reasons Why You Should Call Your Mom." Psychology Today, April 16, 2021. https://www.psychologytoday.com/us/blog/the-psychology-of-relationships/202104/two-key-reasons-why-you-should-call-your-mom.

108   Satya Doyle Byock, Quarterlife: The Search for Self in Early Adulthood (New York: Avery, 2020).

109 Winthrop, Jesse and Anderson, Jenny, The Disengaged Teen: Helping Your Child Learn to Live and Love Better (New York: Crown, 2025).

110 Bowler, Kate. "Lisa Damour: How to Talk to Teenagers," Everything Happens with Kate Bowler, May 6, 2025.

111 QuarterLife Center. "Quarterlife Crisis: Yes, It's a Real Thing." Accessed November 5, 2025. https://quarterlifecenter.com/quarterlife-crisis-yes-real-thing/.

112 Mallom (interview with author, April 23, 2025).

113 Sydnee (interview with author, July 30, 2025).

114 Schoen, John. "70% of College Seniors with Loans Say Debt will Influence Their Career." CNBC, August 29, 2023. https://www.cnbc.com/2023/08/29/70percent-of-college-seniors-with-loans-say-debt-will-influence-their-career.html.

115 Board of Governors of the Federal Reserve System. "Economic Well-Being of U.S. Households in 2024: Higher Education and Student Loans." May 2025. https://www.federalreserve.gov/publications/2025-economic-well-being-of-us-households-in-2024-higher-education-and-student-loans.htm.

116 Deloitte. "Gen Z and Millennial Survey 2024." Accessed November 5, 2025. https://www.deloitte.com/global/en/issues/work/genz-millennial-survey.html.

117 Deja White (interview with author, June 13, 2025).

118 U.S. Department of the Treasury. "Rent, House Prices, and Demographics." Featured Stories. Accessed November 5, 2025. https://home.treasury.gov/news/featured-stories/rent-house-prices-and-demographics.

119 U.S. Census Bureau. "Population Projections." Accessed November 5, 2025. https://www.census.gov/programs-surveys/popproj.html.

120 Loo, Kelly and Wendy Manning. "Young Adults in the Parental Home: 2007–2023." Family Profiles, FP-24-02. Bowling Green State University, National Center for Family & Marriage Research, January 2024. https://www.bgsu.edu/ncfmr/resources/data/family-profiles/loo-young-adults-in-the-parental-home-2007-2023-fp-24-02.html

121 Statistics Canada. "The Daily: Census in Brief: Living Arrangements of Young Adults." Last modified September 19, 2012. https://www12.statcan.gc.ca/census-recensement/2011/as-sa/98-312-x/98-312-x2011003_3-eng.cfm.

122 Henry (interview with author, June 13, 2025).

123 Xoshil (interview with author, May 3, 2025).

124 Pew Research Center. "Decline of Christianity in the U.S. Has Slowed, May Have Leveled Off." February 26, 2025. https://www.pewresearch.org/religion/2025/02/26/decline-of-christianity-in-the-us-has-slowed-may-have-leveled-off/.

125 Haugen, Paul. "Religious Trends Among College Students." Paper presented at the MSW Student Research Conference, University of the Pacific, Stockton, CA, 2025. https://scholarlycommons.pacific.edu/cgi/viewcontent.cgi?article=1017&context=msw-conference.

126 Schlott, Rikki. "Gen Z is more depressed than ever—but these Zoomers reveal their secrets to staying happy." New York Post, May 26, 2025. https://nypost.com/2025/05/26/lifestyle/gen-z-is-more-depressed-than-ever-but-these-zoomers-reveal-their-secrets-to-staying-happy/.

127 Schlott, Vandell, "Gen Z is more depressed."

128 American Psychological Association. "Stress in America: Generation Z, Millennials, and Young Adults' Worries." Accessed November 5, 2025. https://www.apa.org/topics/stress/generation-z-millennials-young-adults-worries.

129 Mayo Clinic Health System. "3 health benefits of volunteering." Accessed November 5, 2025. https://www.mayoclinichealthsystem.org/hometown-health/speaking-of-health/3-health-benefits-of-volunteering.

130 U.S. Bureau of Labor Statistics. "Nonprofits in the Business Employment Dynamics (BED) data." Accessed November 5, 2025. https://www.bls.gov/bdm/nonprofits/nonprofits.htm.

131 Max (interview with Alexa Cole, May 7, 2025).

132 Misha Leybovich (interview with author, August 30, 2025).

133 Global Entrepreneurship Monitor (GEM) Consortium. "New GEM USA Report Highlights Increases in Entrepreneurship and Startup Intentions." November 7, 2024. https://www.gemconsortium.org/news/new-gem-usa-report-highlights-increases-in-entrepreneurship-and-startup-intentions.

134 Whop. "Teen Digital Earnings Report 2024." Accessed November 5, 2025. https://whop.com/blog/teen-digital-earnings-report-2024/.

135 Fickling, David. "Gen Alpha's Dream Careers Are YouTuber, Influencer, and Social Media." Fortune, April 18, 2025. https://fortune.com/article/gen-alpha-dream-careers-youtuber-influencer-social-media/.

136 Doe, Brianna. "007 | Inside My Career Toolbox: Must-Have Platforms & Tools." LinkedIn post, October 24, 2024. https://www.linkedin.com/pulse/007-inside-my-career-toolbox-must-have-platforms-tools-brianna-doe-qxxwc.

137 Erickson Coaching Romania, "What is Solution-Focused Coaching. And what it's not!," blog post, Erickson Coaching Romania, 2021, https://erickson-coaching.ro/what-is-solution-focused-coaching-and-what-its-not/.

138 "Rich Litvin: An Insight into Coaching," March 14, 2022, https://podcasts.apple.com/gb/podcast/rich-litvin-an-insight-into-coaching/id1548923376?i=1000553984109

139 Mike Connolly (interview with author, July 28, 2025).

Research Appendix

Navigating the Quarterlife Career Crisis includes analysis and insights developed via a proprietary survey fielded by the author. The research methodology is outlined below for reference.

**Survey conducted between June 6, 2025 and July 8, 2025
Total Respondents (n = 400)**

**DEMOGRAPHICS
In what year were you born?**

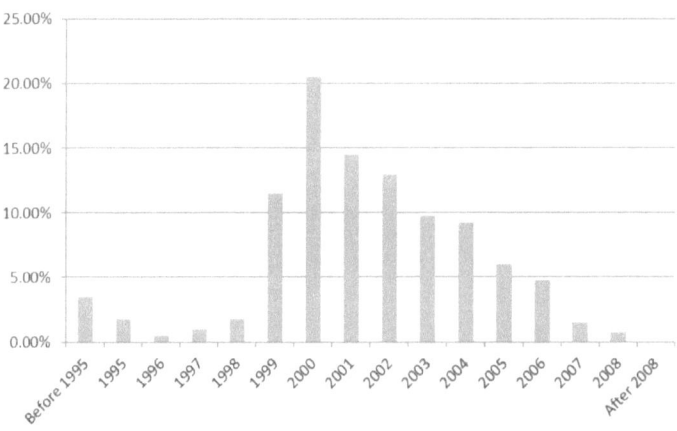

What is your gender?

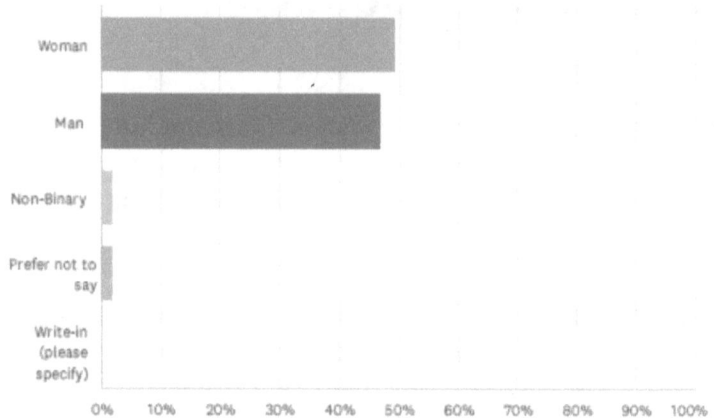

What is your level of education completed?

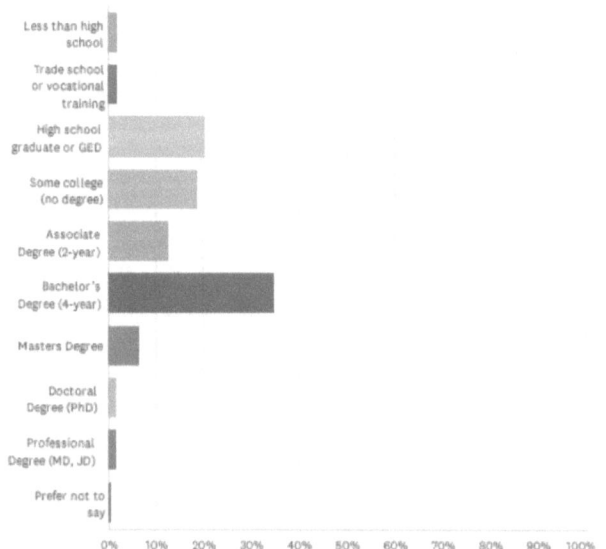

What is your race or origin? (Select one or more boxes)

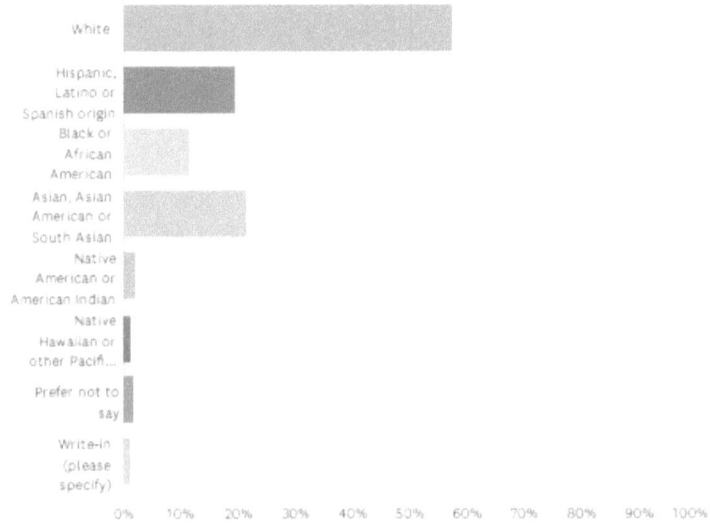

Household Income

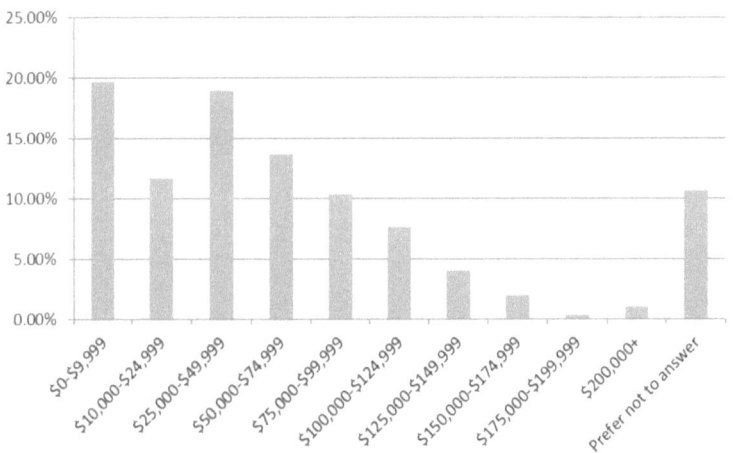

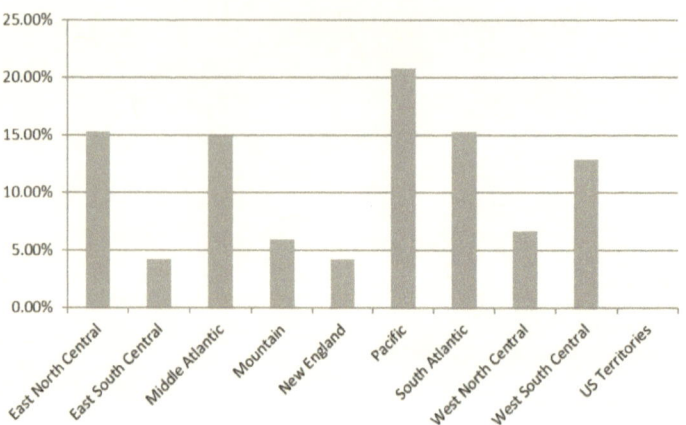

US Geographic Region

Consolidated Resources

Organizations

1. 21st Century Leaders
2. All Saints Career Ministry
3. Amazing If
4. America on Tech
5. Arena
6. Breakroom Buddha
7. The Collaborative
8. Crossroads Career
9. Erickson Coaching International
10. International Coaching Federation
11. Introships
12. Jewish Family & Career Services
13. Job Corps
14. Project Wall Street
15. Tutoring By A College Professor

Books

1. Albrecht, Adam. *What Does Your Fortune Cookie Say?: 80 Important Life Lessons The Universe Is Trying To Share With You.* Ripples Media, 2021.
2. Byock, Satya Doyle. *Quarterlife: The Search for Self in Early Adulthood.* New York: Avery, 2020.
3. Buettner, Dan. *The Blue Zones: Lessons for Living Longer From the People Who've Lived the Longest.* Washington, D.C.: National Geographic, 2008.
4. Burnett, Bill, and Dave Evans. *Designing Your Life:*

How to Build a Well-Lived, Joyful Life. New York: Knopf, 2016.
5. Damour, Lisa. *The Emotional Lives of Teenagers: Raising Connected, Capable, and Compassionate Adolescents.* New York: Ballantine Books, 2023.
6. Elmore, Tim, and Andrew McPeak. Generation Z Unfiltered: Facing Nine Hidden Challenges of the Most Anxious Population. Poet Gardener Publishing, 2019.
7. Haidt, Jonathan. *Anxious Generation: How the Great Rewiring of Childhood Is Causing an Epidemic of Mental Illness.* New York: Penguin Press, 2024.
8. Hartz, John. *Failureship.* Place of publication not specified: John Hartz, 2023.
9. Holiday, Ryan. *The Obstacle Is the Way: The Timeless Art of Turning Trials into Triumph.* New York: Portfolio/Penguin, 2014.
10. Jay, Meg. *The Defining Decade: Why Your Twenties Matter—And How to Make the Most of Them Now.* New York: Twelve, 2012.
11. LeSourd, Cate. *Coming of Age: Our Journey Into Adulthood.* Oakdale Publishing Group LLC: Cate LeSourd, 2023.
12. Robbins, Alexandra, and Abby Wilner. *Quarterlife Crisis: The Unique Challenges of Life in Your Twenties.* New York: Tarcher/Putnam, 2001.
13. Tupper, Helen, and Sarah Ellis. *Squiggly Career: Ditch the Ladder, Discover Opportunity, Design Your Career.* New York: Portfolio/Penguin, 2020.
14. Yeager, David. *10 to 25: The Science of Motivating Young People.* New York: Scribner, 2024.
15. Young Rivers, Stacey. *Career Smarts for College Students: A Practical Career Guide for Work in the Age of AI.* Self-published, 2023.

CareerTok

@careercoachmandy (Mandy Tang)
Columbia MBA and career coach offering guidance on job changes, career pivots, and professional development.

@allifromcorporate0 (Allison Peck)
Specializes in helping early-career STEM professionals with job hunting, interviewing, and networking.

@rawantheplug (Rawan):
Rawan is noted for her supportive approach, especially toward underrepresented communities and those navigating stressful career transitions. She creates content that acknowledges the emotional challenges of job searching and workplace stress.

@CareerConfident (Gabrielle Woody):
Gabrielle Woody is highlighted for her inclusive, supportive content. She addresses not just practical career advice but also the emotional impact of workplace discrimination and stress, offering guidance on how to respond and cope.

@roxycouse:
Focuses on first-generation college students, offering support and advice for those unsure about their career trajectory.

Exercises

Ikigai

The ikigai model is a foundation for internal exploration that illuminates the intersection between four categories: Strengths, Interests, Demand, and What the World Needs.

This process involves a journaling exercise of the four areas and some meaningful contemplation or discussion of the output. I have found this modest effort can lead to useful new sparks that may light the way toward previously latent professional pursuits.

Note: Each area should be completed independently. For example, the demand column is to identify areas of macro growth in a particular industry, function or geography. This does not have to immediately align with your existing skills or interests.

Once you complete the table above, consider these follow-up questions:

1. What topics show up more than once?

2. What are your takeaways?

3. How might you come up with some additional answers?

4. How can your insights be applied to your exploration process?

FIGure it Out

Beginning with my job search process after graduating from business school in 2003, this proprietary framework has evolved over the last twenty years to become the FIGure it Out method. This method can help you develop an intentional company target list that focuses your energy and optimizes your opportunities. The FIGure it Out moniker identifies Function, Industry, and Geography as the main variables involved in filtering your career path possibilities.

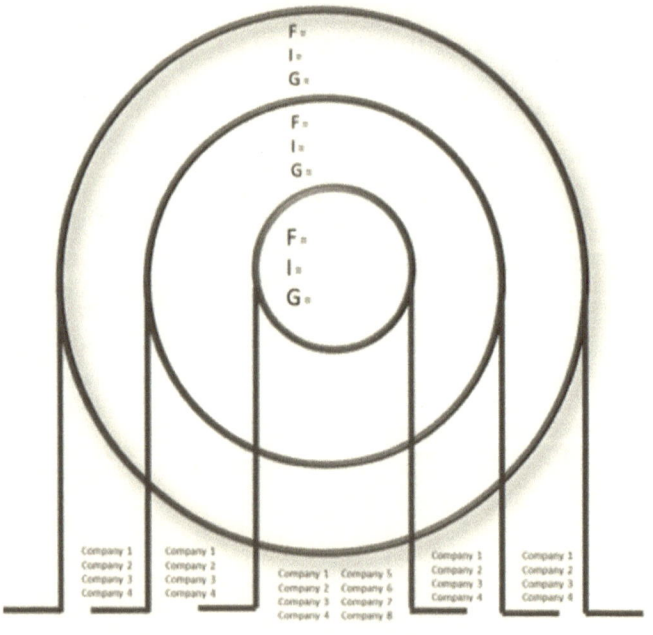

Complete each ring:

1. Ring 1 is your bullseye target

2. List one or two elements for each parameter

3. Determine relative flexibility to create outer rings

4. List five to ten target companies for each ring

5. Prioritize your time accordingly for optimal strategy

Personal Board of Advisors

Having a personal board of advisors can help you make big decisions in your life and career. This select group of confidants can be there for you when you want to dig into your thoughts about your current situation and discuss alternatives.

Here are a few archetypes that can help you identify three to five people who can be valuable sounding boards:

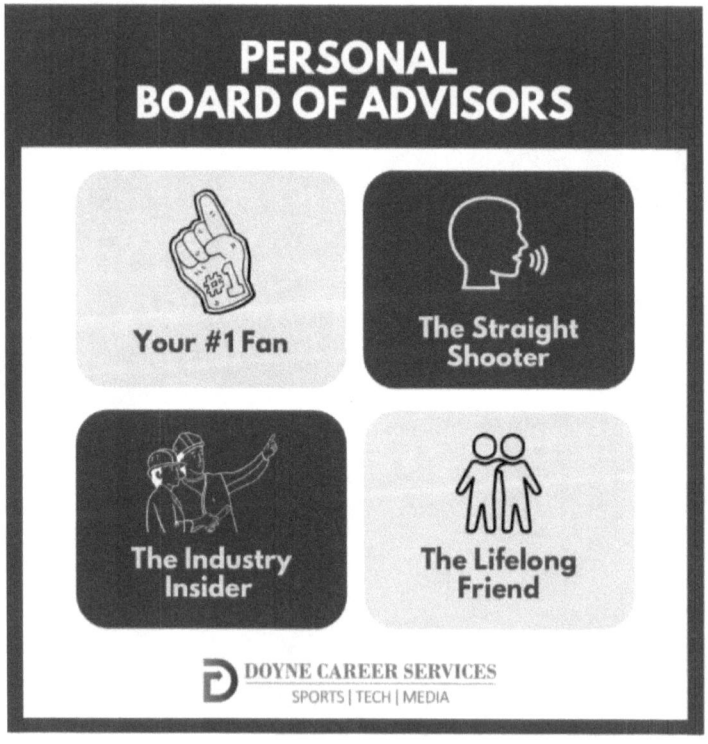

Your #1 Fan. During a difficult time, it's essential to give yourself a solid foundation. Leaning on someone who holds you in high regard will support your self-esteem and give you the confidence to propel yourself toward a better situation.

The Straight Shooter. This person tells it like it is. The truth-teller can break through your defense mechanisms to get an important point across that you may not want to hear but you need to hear.

The Industry Insider. Your industry or functional specialty may have nuances that are difficult for people outside of that area to understand. Even if you want to shift your career in another direction, this empathetic advisor can help you assess the current crisis level.

The Lifelong Friend. Having someone by your side who understands your values is critical to cutting through the chaos and reminding you what matters most as you make difficult decisions.

Of course, trust and discretion are valuable characteristics of each candidate. Ideally, they are great listeners who are dependable and devoted to helping you find what's right for you. If you find yourself short on options, a career coach can help.

Additional Exercises

ICAN - Networking Strategy and Action Plan - see Chapter 6

Level Up on LinkedIn - see Chapter 9

AI Tools for Career Transition - see Chapter 10

Ready, Set, Go! A Startup Process with an Action Bias - see Chapter 16

Self-Assessments

Sabateur Assessment - Identify your top derailers

16 Personalities - Strengths assessment, derived from the Myers-Briggs Type Indicator (MBTI)

DiSC Assessment - Workplace behavior type

Emotional Intelligence - EQ self-assessment

About the Author

Scott Doyne is an ICF-certified career coach and bestselling author who transforms career anxiety into clarity. After 20 years at Turner Sports, rising from intern to SVP, leading digital innovation for NASCAR and the NBA—including earning an Emmy for technological innovation—he left corporate life to dedicate himself to coaching. He's now delivered over 1,200 hours of coaching, helping clients land roles at top companies like Amazon, Apple, and Disney. A sought-after keynote speaker, he has delivered workshops and keynotes to global audiences. He is also the author of the *Career Crisis Series*, including *Exploring the Midlife Career Crisis* and *Navigating the Quarterlife Career Crisis*. Scott lives in Atlanta with his wife where they raised two children and their beloved Goldendoodle, Baxter.

www.ingramcontent.com/pod-product-compliance
Lightning Source LLC
LaVergne TN
LVHW040046080526
838202LV00045B/3505